Children's Rooms and Play Areas

Joseph F. Schram and John Boeschen

Ideals Publishing Corp.
Milwaukee, Wisconsin

Table of Contents

Introduction **3**

The Child's Bedroom **4**

Furniture for Children **12**

The Bathroom **17**

Retreats—Attics, Basements, Studies **21**

Storage **31**

Noise Control and Lighting **50**

Attractive Sturdy Floors **55**

Wall and Window Treatment **58**

Play Areas—Indoors and Out **65**

Safety **94**

Index **96**

ISBN 0-8249-6119-6

Copyright © 1982 by Joseph F. Schram and John Boeschen

Published by Ideals Publishing Corporation
11315 Watertown Plank Road
Milwaukee, Wisconsin 53226

Editor, David Schansberg

⌂ SUCCESSFUL
HOME IMPROVEMENT SERIES

Bathroom Planning and Remodeling
Kitchen Planning and Remodeling
Space Saving Shelves and Built-ins
Finishing Off Additional Rooms
Finding and Fixing the Older Home
Money Saving Home Repair Guide
Homeowner's Guide to Tools
Homeowner's Guide to Electrical Wiring
Homeowner's Guide to Plumbing
Homeowner's Guide to Roofing and Siding
Homeowner's Guide to Fireplaces
Home Plans for the '80s
Planning and Building Home Additions
Homeowner's Guide to Concrete and Masonry
Homeowner's Guide to Landscaping
Homeowner's Guide to Swimming Pools
Homeowner's Guide to Fastening Anything
Planning and Building Vacation Homes
Homeowner's Guide to Floors and Staircases
Home Appliance Repair Guide
Homeowner's Guide to Wood Refinishing
Children's Rooms and Play Areas
Wallcoverings: Paneling, Painting, and Papering
Money Saving Natural Energy Systems
How to Build Your Own Home

Introduction

For the past twenty-five years, the American home buyer has been offered a glittering array of new products, materials, and designs in single-family homes. Through all of this, perhaps the least consideration has been given to the child's role in a home. Think for a moment of the model homes you have visited, and you will quickly recall that the selling emphasis has always been placed on the beautiful modern kitchen, the lavish bathroom, and the adult-oriented master bedroom suite "where you can close the door and get away from the children". Few in the housing industry have concentrated their talents in the direction of the child's spaces in the home. They have left selecting the necessary furniture and accessories for the child's room, which is generally the smallest, entirely up to you.

Educators stress that parents can create better learning environments for their children at home by encouraging their independence. This may even begin with placing food and drink on a low shelf in the refrigerator so that when a young child wants food he can help himself. It continues as we arrange the home environment in such a way that children can take care of themselves and their activities instead of requiring constant adult assistance.

Children's Rooms and Play Areas will assist you in understanding the basic planning and building of home spaces for children.

There is no better person than you to determine exactly what your children need in your home since you are aware of their likes and dislikes, their needs, their goals, and, most importantly, their daily routines. With the material presented here you should be able to match each child to a more pleasant surrounding, one he or she can be comfortable in.

Builders and designers will tell you without reservation that there is a demand today for more practical space division of the home. Both children and adults are asking for more separation to pursue individual pastimes in leisure hours. Add to this demand the fact that today's children have become loaded with their own special possessions—their clothes, elaborate and enormous toys, and educational equipment—and you will see why it is difficult to get two or three fully-equipped children into just one bedroom.

The Child's Bedroom

Of all the areas within the home that can be set apart for our youngsters—whether infant, child, or teenager—the bedroom offers the most opportunities for contribution to the young person's development, personality, growth, and self-expression. The knowledge that he or she possesses a personal territorial space can positively affect emotional outlook.

Furniture designers who in the past have designed the child's bedroom have, for the most part, merely redesigned and scaled down adult rooms. Interior designers have devoted their efforts to the master bedroom (where more expensive furniture can be utilized) while the children's rooms accepted hand-me-down furniture from early days of marriage or bargains from a variety of sources. Many designers now are beginning to depart from this tradition in order to create children's rooms that are oriented more toward the needs of their occupants.

Noted West Coast designer Marlene Grant, for example, firmly believes the child's bedroom should be dramatically changed to what children would find comfortable during their three age cycles: birth to seven years, eight through twelve years, and teenage to departure from the parents' home. Mrs. Grant speaks for a growing number of designers who believe placing a baby in a 10' × 12' room with an 8-foot ceiling and a crib as large as a single adult bed unnecessarily creates fear in the child. She rightly asks how an adult would feel sleeping in the middle of a gymnasium.

Child Level

Studies conducted at Stanford University's renowned Bing Nursery School clearly illustrate that child-level furnishings create a better place to grow and learn. High chairs (dangerous because of the possible damage when an infant falls out), playpens, and cribs have been found to be restraining devices that increase the child's dependency on adults. For both physical and mental health reasons, the answer appears to be better-scaled furniture and surroundings. The room can be allocated into zones to include sleep areas, storage, and play space.

The room, without furnishings, presents a totally different environment to a child than to an adult. The ceilings seem so high that they are almost out of sight, yet these same ceilings serve as the background for the child. Bedrooms and playrooms can become children's rooms by lowering the ceilings, adding lofts, using scaled-down furniture, replacing the forbidding floor-to-ceiling door with Dutch-style doors, careful color selection for specific sections of the room, and placement of pillows and shelves at child level. Ceilings which normally measure 8 feet in height can easily be lowered to a more proportionate 5 or 6 feet for children by attaching parachutes or double sheets around the walls and creating a new, soft, lower ceiling. At the same time, a comfortable area that has been furnished with pillows and screened off from the rest of the room can effectively communicate a sense of quiet to children that will encourage them to relax at rest time.

Many child experts believe that children should be taught to recognize sleepiness and should be encouraged to initiate their own naps. In safe and accessible environments, children can learn to initiate behavior without constantly seeking help or adult approval. These same experts believe parents need to stop doing everything so their children will learn to judge accurately for themselves.

Basics for Smaller Sizing Most studies related to bedroom planning specify the same basics as set forth by the government in HUD's Minimum Property Standards. Among these basics are the following requirements for properly designed children's rooms:

- a minimum wall length of 8 feet, with greater length desirable for better furniture placement;
- a minimum 32-inch-wide entry door at standard 80-inch height;
- at least one outside window with sill height no more than 4 feet from the floor, the openable area of window not less than 5 square feet with no dimension less than 22 inches.
- a minimum 36-inch closet rod length for one-person secondary bedroom and 60-inch rod length for a two-person room.

The other two most important dimensions to keep in mind in planning any bedroom arrangement are 28 inches and 40 inches. Both dimensions relate specifically to bed placement, with the lesser dimension being the distance between the bed and a wall; the 40 inches is the space needed between either the foot of the bed or the other side of the bed and the facing opposite wall, furniture, or closet front. The 28-inch dimension is also the distance recommended between twin beds.

Most modern bedrooms have been designed with the entry door located no more than 24 inches from the corner of the room in order to avoid interference with

Plastics play an important role in this attic hideaway. The lightweight furniture, storage-bunk, and wall-hung play table free up extra space in a small room. The washable wallcoverings are strippable and vinyl coated. Photo courtesy of Imperial Wallcoverings

furniture. Keep in mind that in-swinging doors require a minimum 32-inch arc space from hinged jamb to latch jamb. When the door is placed 24 inches from the room corner, a special hinge stop can be used to limit the door swing and to permit furniture placement in that 2-foot area.

A later chapter deals specifically with children's furniture, but your planning will most certainly involve the following minimum mattress sizes:

Crib	27 × 48 inches
Twin	39 × 75 inches
Full	54 × 75 inches
Long Twin	39 × 80 inches
Long Full	54 × 80 inches

Child-Oriented Adaptations

Younger Years The use of Dutch doors enables parents to close the lower section so the child feels he is on his own, while the top half can be left open so that parents can unobtrusively check in frequently.

Carpeted cylinders and platforms are excellent for a young child's room. These elements can help identify a play section or, equipped with a pad, signal a sleep area. Boxes and cubicles into which children may shove their toys will more readily prompt cleanup than will conventional dressers and drawers.

Designer Grant stresses the use of the cool colors on the color wheel and shuns wild graphics for the sleep section of a young child's room. Likewise, she recommends the use of smooth carpet squares to provide a reassuring warm surface and blinds which permit to-

This bedroom, created for a thirteen-year-old girl, uses a blue and red floral fabric to set the mood. The canopied bed was easily created with a length of fabric and dowels suspended from the ceiling. The fabric is repeated on closet doors and on the walls where the reversed wainscoting features richly grained paneling. Photo courtesy of Masonite Corporation

tal blockout of daylight. She and others point to allergy problems which can occur with shag carpeting and draperies that gather dust.

As the child reaches six or seven years of age, parents are much more aware of his interests and can help to direct him in the selection of bedroom furnishings. Again, programming the room for varied activities is highly desirable. The child's interests, whether animals, camping, athletics, or other topics, should be considered when selecting wallcoverings.

Lofts in a child's room permit some privacy and provide a quiet space for reading or thinking. They also give children a unique opportunity to get a new look at their world, looking down instead of up; the loft allows them to see the world from a different angle. It can be considered a very private, special retreat from the family.

Teenage Years Much can be said for totally turning the room over to a teenager for decorating and arranging. The scene may be totally foreign to adult tastes, with posters on every inch of ceiling and items strung from every corner; but the total environment is

Converting a Sun Porch into a Bedroom

Converting a combination sun porch and summer bedroom in an older home to an attractive year-round bedroom can be carried out successfully and inexpensively if the homeowner keeps an open mind to designer recommendations, has the patience and ability to do some of the work himself, and carefully evaluates the costs of alternative materials. The original sun porch had several architectural problems that creative use of paneling and wallcovering would correct. A French door was selected to complement the only mandatory requirement for the room—a canopy bed for the family's pre-teen daughter. Structural problems were tackled by the entire family. Rotted wood was torn out, primarily from around the windows. Outside shingles that were nailed to one side were removed. Two windows were eliminated, and the outside closure was patched with materials to match the rest of the house. Everything else was stripped down to the bare wood. Rough surfaces left by removing the shingles, plus the room's lack of insulation, led to the decision to panel wherever possible. Insulation was added; then prefinished hardboard paneling reflecting a country French design was installed. Each panel has three long, narrow panel sections, 16 inches wide. This modular design was utilized effectively by cutting the panels lengthwise and installing the 16-inch sections between two windows along one wall and between a window and two shadow boxes that were built into the adjoining wall. A patterned wallcovering was used on the ceiling, valances,

and lower walls. Cutouts from the wallcovering were glued to the window shades to enhance the pattern. Netting and simple uprights created the four-poster canopy effect at a much lower cost. Carpeting, new lighting, and a combination of new and old furniture completed the project.

A fabulous wood cutout of a tree decorates this room. You can create your own cutout design. Photo courtesy of American Plywood Association

A wood feature-wall in this youngster's room includes a handy storage unit with adjustable shelves that can be rearranged to suit the changing needs of your child. Photo courtesy of Western Wood Products Association

individualistic, and parental approval expresses a great deal of love and acceptance of the child and his ability to make decisions of his own.

Room Location

Children's bedrooms may come in all shapes and sizes, but in most instances they are referred to in the housing industry as secondary rooms. They are generally smaller than most other rooms in the home. Long rectangular rooms can be made square in appearance through color selection and furniture placement, just as narrow rooms can be made to appear wider by means of decorating techniques.

Unless you are planning a new home, the location of your child's bedroom has probably already been determined, and there is little you can do to change this situation. In planning a new home, however, follow the advice of experts and keep the bedroom wing separate from the more noisy sections containing kitchen, family room, and living room.

It is also recommended that bedrooms be as convenient as possible to separate or family bathrooms. Many efficient floor plans incorporate a bathroom between two bedrooms, with easy access from both rooms and the hallway.

Depending upon the age of the occupant, proximity

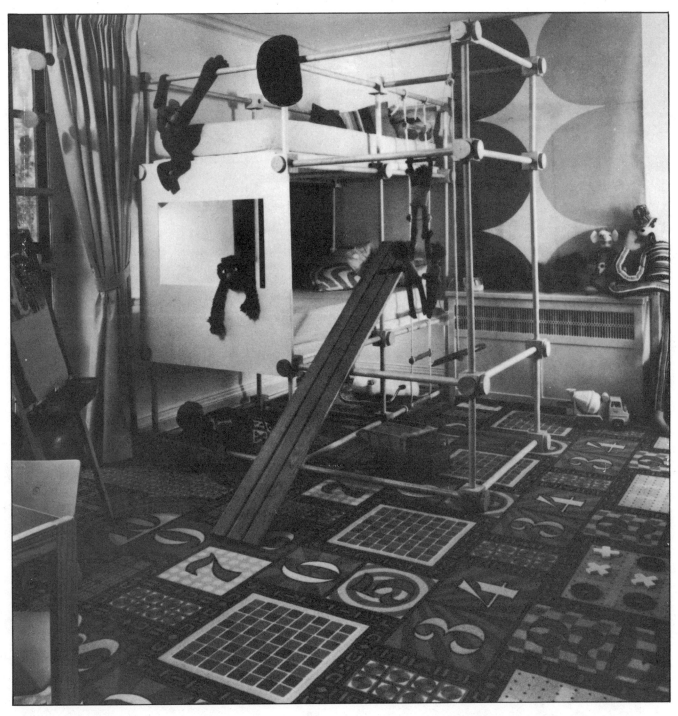

of the child's bedroom to the parents' master bedroom varies in importance. Most agree that when children are young it is more important that their bedrooms be near that of their parents. As they become teens, it is highly desirable that distance exist to lessen the sound of the television, stereo, or other audible background.

Wonder Walls

Accessories enable the homeowner to radically change the theme of a child's bedroom in relatively little time and with very little cost. Sheets, specifically, need not be restricted to the bed, for they can be

Home-assembled furniture adds considerably to the enjoyment of a child's room. Units such as these save valuable floor space by placing bunks above play areas. Note vertical rails that prevent the youngsters from falling off the top bunk. The floor is carpeted and provides an instant warm play surface. Photo courtesy of Jorges Carpet Mills, Inc.

used on walls, a movable screen, a sofa, or even a lampshade. Sheets can satisfy the longing for something new and different each season of the year. Major manufacturers offer booklets containing literally hundreds of ideas for room transformations using this kind of colorful fabric. Martex™, for example, suggests that entire walls can be quickly covered by putting the

sheets up with a staple gun. Wallpaper adhesive can be used for a more permanent application.

Shirred Sheets To cover a wall with shirred sheets, measure the width and multiply that by two and one-half. Measure the height, add one inch at either end, and then add another inch and one-half to make a one-inch casing. Stitch the casing, and thread it with string or cable cord. Attach the fabric with staple gun at one end of the wall. Do the same at the other end. Adjust gathers. Use the staple gun horizontally starting at the top center, one inch at a time, working each direction alternately out to the sides. Repeat for the bottom.

A change in decor using basically the same furnishings enables you to easily update a child's bedroom as he or she grows. The first arrangement (left) shows how flexible modulars and homemade plywood cubes fill a young child's storage and play neds. The cubes were covered by priming the raw wood, applying wallcovering, and then coating with clear polyurethane. Window shades were dressed up with cutouts of Raggedy Ann and Andy. In reworking the same room (below), wallcoverings in a sophisticated pastel reflect a teenager's tastes. The cubes have now been stacked under a board to make a desk and hold plants and a TV. The cubes hold snacks for friends, and the dressers line up as a headboard for the bed. Simple plywood cornices cut in points are set over green window shades. Photos courtesy of Imperial Wallcoverings

Hanging Blankets Dramatic blanket throws are more frequently used on the wall as a focal point. Lions, elephants, horses, pandas, tigers, and other animals are very popular with the young child. Still other children's blanket prints feature cartoon characters, sports heroes, or movie themes.

Alphabet Stencils This wall treatment is especially appealing to the young child. It takes little more than a base coat of white and a few pints of assorted primary colors. If you don't want to permanently decorate your wall, attach a floor-to-ceiling roll of paper.

- Tools and materials—11 × 14-inch cardboard for stencils; smaller stencil set to use as a guide; white paint for the background; pints of red, yellow and blue paint; mixing pails; stiff-bristled brushes or foam brushes; masking tape.
- Variations—Try whatever color scheme you and your child prefer. For example, you might use blue, turquoise, and green as the main colors with accents of yellow; or, for a more grown-up graphic look, stencil in a single color, such as brown.

Cutouts The tree silhouette cut from wood shown in the picture is an unusual decoration for a child's room. If forestry doesn't appeal to your child, use the same technique to create other favorite objects, such as circus clowns, cars, a castle, or animals. Plans are available from the American Plywood Association.

Tools and materials required to make a cutout include: one sheet of ¼-inch APA grade-trademarked plywood; brown and green wood stain; coping saw; large sheet of brown wrapping paper; sandpaper; adhesive; nails.

Following are the steps required to make a cutout tree:

1. Design a free-form tree, following the rough outline of the tree illustrated. The trunk is one piece; the treetop is another. Added contrasting areas in the treetop are separate pieces of plywood.
2. Draw and cut out the tree once you have designed it on kraft paper. Position it on the wall and make whatever adjustments are necessary to have it fill the space.
3. Using your kraft paper pattern, fit the pieces on the plywood sheet and outline them. Cut out pieces.
4. Sand edges and lightly sand the front surface.
5. Following the stain manufacturer's instructions, experiment with scrap plywood to achieve the depth of stain you need for tree parts. For instance, you may want to use two coats to create a dark green for the treetop and edges of branches

One family's approach to decorating a teenage boy's room began with the selection of wall paneling to serve as a backdrop for posters and other display items such as models and trophies. The decorative wall is hardboard, which simulates cork. Next came the furniture selection, which includes a corner colonial-style dresser and desk with matching freestanding shelf unit. A light contrasting shag carpet offsets the heavy look of the dark furniture. At this point the teenager used his own creativity in hanging model airplanes from the ceiling, displaying miniature motorcycles on the desk and shelves, and adding the many accents that make the room.

on the treetop; and only one coat of lighter green for the branch clusters.

6. Stain all the sections; allow to dry.
7. Attach branch clusters to the treetop with panel adhesive or nails. If you use brads or nails, paint the heads so they won't show.
8. Attach the tree trunk to the wall with either nails or adhesive, then attach the treetop. (Nailing the tree into a stud will allow the easiest removal when you wish to make a change.)

Furniture for Children

A casual tour of any of the large furniture stores or merchandise marts located in major cities will quickly provide you with a plentiful array of furniture for children's rooms. Some of the pieces seem ageless, for they have been manufactured for many years with little revision in design. Other items are surprisingly new and interesting, such as the Cubo, a roll-up foam unit which instantly converts from seating to sleeping purposes. The pillow unit is used partially open for watching TV, but when it is opened flat, it will sleep an adult.

The bulk of the furniture purchased in America for use by children finds its place in the bedroom. A simple nursery with basic pieces can cost $500; a teen's more formal seven or eight-piece selection can exceed $1,000. Departures from these ordinary selections, however, can provide the unusual, the more interesting, the more enjoyable, and sometimes the least expensive alternative.

Furniture can strongly influence a child. The California School of Design, San Francisco, best capsulizes the importance of furniture by telling students "we eat, sleep, work, play, love, store, watch, listen, and display all human activity in relation to furniture."

You can use furniture all day, every day. You also see it in quantity; while you are using one piece, you are seeing many other pieces. Our concept of the furniture's appearance, combined with its use, constitutes a major factor in choosing those pieces our children may live with for years.

Few of us live the way our parents did, and this change has brought about new furniture that we may not have even recognized as new. Examples of such furniture are the television stand, chairs that fit the body, waterbeds, foam cushions, molded plastics and plywood, and built-in furniture. At the same time, furniture which was popular with our parents is making a resurgence such as items made of wicker and rattan.

Most interior designers build their business on their ability to search out furniture and accessories that are unusual and are more interesting than buying a set or a suite. You have this same opportunity in your child's room, and children will often share your enthusiasm for finding furniture that best fits the environment and the child.

Choosing Furniture

The obvious first consideration in choosing furniture for a child's room is his age. Adult-size furniture is almost certain to create frustration. A chest-on-chest is great for an adult, but serves little purpose for a child who has to climb on a chair each time to get to the top drawers and their contents. Likewise, few children are comfortable if they have to kneel on a chair to use an adult-height desk 27 to 29 inches off the floor.

Many educators and interior designers believe the best place for the young child is the floor itself. Here a platform unit can be constructed to serve as a bed and

Chest beds offer various storage arrangements for a child's clothing, books, and toys. Pictured here are a bed that combines drawers with movable shelves and a bed with three spacious drawers. Photos courtesy of Bassett Furniture Industries

Valuable floor space in the bedroom can be saved with Toob-line System furniture designed for youngsters. This arrangement places the desk and dresser beneath the loft-bed. Other arrangements permit a second bed placed either parallel to the loft-bed or at a right angle to it, but still allow space for a desk. Most system groupings can be arranged to suit individual needs and preferences. Photo courtesy of HUDDLE

storage unit and can be used for playtime as well. Another possibility is to totally eliminate a bed in favor of a roll-up unit much akin to the familiar sleeping bag. There are few mother-child arguments about making the bed when one need merely roll it up and place it in the corner, and the floor space gained creates more room for play.

Well-planned closets can help reduce the need for dresser and chest space. Clear plastic drawers are now available at many discount department stores in a wide range of sizes. These make it easier for the child to find what he is seeking. These drawers can be a lower part of the main clothes closet during the child's younger years and later rearranged as the child gets older.

Bunk beds can be purchased with or without a trundle bed to accommodate a third person. This unit is 70 inches high.

Types of Construction In considering the purchase of conventional children's furniture, you will encounter three basic construction types: solid wood, wood veneer, and combination plastic laminate-wood. Each, when well-crafted, is adequate for a child's use over a long period of time. There is more furniture of lasting quality made today than ever before. While fine handcrafted furniture is still available, machinery has so thoroughly revolutionized woodworking that it is possible not only to duplicate the perfection of the handcraftsman but also improve upon his results.

Attractive solid woods are used for various types of traditional furniture styles and some modern styles. Furniture frames and the turned, shaped, and carved parts of most furniture styles are generally of solid wood construction.

Conversely, the tops, drawers, fronts, doors, and side and end panels on fine furniture are usually veneered or bonded construction. The high-grade cabinet woods are used chiefly as face veneers, and about 90 percent of all wood furniture produced today involves at least some bonded construction.

Plastic laminates in attractive wood-grain patterns as well as solid colors are also common today. Intricate drawer and cabinet faces of molded plastic bring the richness of handcrafting within the means of most homeowners. Molded plastic drawers are particularly desirable in children's rooms.

Furniture Pieces—Nursery In purchasing furniture for a nursery, you'll want to consider the following items:

- *Crib*—Usually 53 × 30 inches, 45 to 48 inches high, with both side rails lowerable, plastic free-wheeling casters, adjustable springs, and plastic teething rails. Cribs today must meet Crib Safety Standards as published in the Federal Register. Many specialists recommend, however, that the child be moved from a crib as soon as he begins to climb to prevent the possibility of his falling. Low boxbeds with side rails that keep the child from rolling out are preferable once the child becomes active.

- *Dresser*—Usually with three or more drawers, often with durable plastic laminate top equipped with soft pad and safety strap (for diapering). Height is generally 31 inches while width varies from approximately 42 to 62 inches, with an 18-inch depth.

- *Chest*—Approximately 41 to 50 inches high, four or more drawers, approximately 32 to 37 inches wide, and 18 inches deep. Many dressers and chests have a baked-on finish, some have dovetail drawers and center drawer guides for longer wear.

Waterbeds Waterbed systems have been designed as standard children's beds and cribs. While most furniture pieces used by children have been created and designed by adults, there is one notable exception—the waterbed. A student at San Francisco State University, Charles Hall, is widely credited with being the inventor of the first waterbed.

At the beginning there was one basic waterbed. Its mattress consisted simply of a vinyl water-filled bag which was then placed on top of an electric heater and fitted into a box-frame base. That model still exists today under the name of the pure waterbed, with a better grade of vinyl mattress.

There is also the hybrid waterbed. The difference between most hybrids and the pure waterbed is the lack of a heater in the hybrid. There is, instead, an insulator pad which protects the sleeper from the water's chill and a foam frame which holds the vinyl water mattress, thus requiring less water while creating a firm edge.

Technological advances are not the only features offered by the waterbeds. Fashion, more apparent than construction, has been equally as inviting. Many manufacturers are now designing frames to match bedroom sets. Their lines range from the traditional to the contemporary. There must be 500 different bed styles on the market today, with the most popular in the $500 price range. Newer waterbed designs closely resemble the traditional mattress and box spring. The liner is encased in a frame which is positioned on top of a heavy-duty box spring.

Hammocks The influence of the sailor's bed is becoming more evident each year as hammocks find their way into children's rooms. The hammock provides an excellent guest bed or lounging area for reading or watching television. The unit is a lot more popular with youngsters than is a regular bed or a folding cot.

Many changes have been made in hammock con-

Conventional nursery furniture usually consists of the three pieces shown here: single dresser with foam pad and safety strap, chest, and crib. Photo courtesy of Bassett Furniture Industries

struction since they hung in the great sailing vessels from the ship's bulkheads or walls. Today's hammock comes in several sizes to accommodate one or more persons. Most units are 11 to 12 feet long, the ends are hung 6 feet 8 inches high, and the center is about 2 feet off the floor. The units stretch slightly in use and conform to your body while providing gentle support. The most comfortable resting position is diagonal so that the body is nearly level. The bed of the hammock can be of familiar rope construction using flexible cotton or nylon, and it may be any color in solids, stripes, and patterns. Prices can range from under $20 to nearly $100, depending upon fabric, construction, and size.

Large hammocks (78 × 140 inches or more) are great for playrooms and outdoor play areas, as they can easily handle four small children simultaneously.

Furniture You Build Yourself

Numerous items have been used by talented persons to create their own furniture, from simple two-drawer steel file cabinets and flush panel doors to create a desk, to large circular tubes for crawl-in relaxing. Chairs, especially, seem to know no limits. Old tractor seats, nail kegs, suspended netting, canvas slings, and other designs can provide adequate seating in a child's room.

Create a Super Block for Two Here is a super system manufactured by the GAF Corporation, in which almost all needs, including sleep, storage, study, and game-playing, are incorporated into one unit. The easy-maintenance vinyl flooring, high-gloss paint, and cotton fabric are all washable. This offers one solution to a tiny room for two tots. The unit provides two beds, a desk/shelf area for two with four drawers each, shelves for games or toys beneath steps, and a unique long storage area.

- Tools and materials—Twelve sheets of 4 foot × 8

Here is an expanded view of the Super Block. This design for sleeping and activities for two uses Gafstar Brite-Bond sheet vinyl in the Bandana pattern. Note that both sleeping areas have guards. Everything is cut from ¾-inch plywood and assembled with simple hand tools. Construction breaks down into three major steps (as shown in the drawing below): assembly of the desk unit, attachment of the sides and bed unit, and installation of the steps and rear wall. Required materials include twelve sheets of 4 × 8-foot plywood, one flush door, nails, glue, and paint. Photo courtesy of GAF Corporation

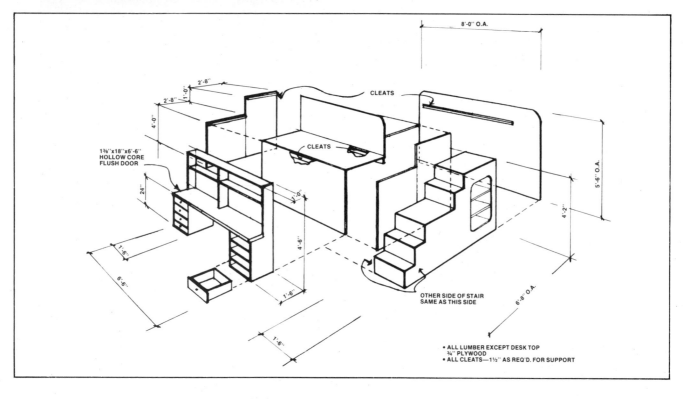

foot × ¾-inch plywood, one good side; one flush door 18 inches × 6 feet 6 inches × 1½ inches or two pieces ¾-inch plywood laminated together (for desk top); eight 1-inch (diameter) wood knobs; 2 × 1½-inch finishing nails; 1¼-inch roundhead wood screws; white glue; wood putty; sandpaper; primer-sealer; enamel; circular handsaw; hand tools for assembly.

Flooring is Gafstar Brite-Bond Citation Collection sheet vinyl in the Bandana pattern. You also will need two standard 75 × 30-inch cot mattresses and bed linens.

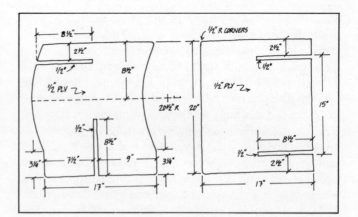

Three Furniture Pieces, One Design Here is a project that the kids can help with, and they will enjoy the finished project for hours at a time. Depending upon which way they stand it, this three-in-one chair can be a rocker, a table, or an everyday chair. Most suitable for younger children, it is one way of providing furniture for modest cost. When youngsters outgrow this furniture, you can consider more permanent furniture to take them through school-age years. The designs are from Georgia-Pacific.

- Tools and materials—One 4 foot × 8 foot × ½-inch plywood panel A-B or A-C grade; fine sandpaper; wood filler; sealer; interior semigloss enamel paint or stain; 8d finishing nails; drill. One plywood panel makes two chairs.

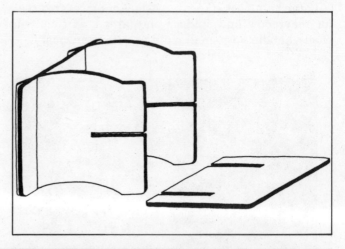

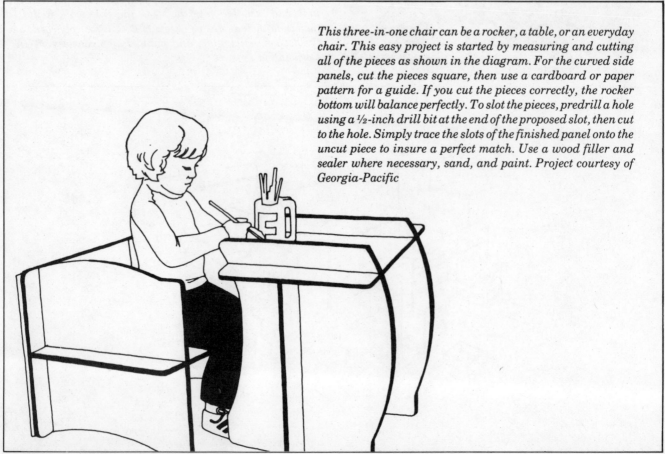

This three-in-one chair can be a rocker, a table, or an everyday chair. This easy project is started by measuring and cutting all of the pieces as shown in the diagram. For the curved side panels, cut the pieces square, then use a cardboard or paper pattern for a guide. If you cut the pieces correctly, the rocker bottom will balance perfectly. To slot the pieces, predrill a hole using a ½-inch drill bit at the end of the proposed slot, then cut to the hole. Simply trace the slots of the finished panel onto the uncut piece to insure a perfect match. Use a wood filler and sealer where necessary, sand, and paint. Project courtesy of Georgia-Pacific

The Bathroom

When it comes to designing and decorating a bathroom primarily for children's use, the overriding factors should be practicality and safety. This room too often is initially planned for adults with little thought, if any, given to its use by youngsters who will be splashing at walls and floors on a daily basis.

Considerable change has been made in the American bathroom, but the least of this change has been directed toward youngsters. Visit any new home development, and you will find master baths with an elegance that helps to sell the house. Such baths are important, but so are those that will be used by children.

While every home cannot be equipped with a separate bathroom for each bedroom, it is highly desirable that a specific bathroom be set aside for children. If the home is small and one bathroom must meet the needs of all, it should be large enough and planned to accommodate more than one person at a time. Such baths can be compartmentalized for desired privacy. A partition which separates the lavatories from the tub/toilet area adds privacy and convenience. Some bathrooms go one step further, with separate private zones for each fixture and a common dressing room. This particular design works extremely well for a large family.

Fixtures

Tubs The bathtub today comes in many styles and sizes, including space-saving corner models, square shapes with circular tub area, deep tubs for steeping comfort, safety tubs with slip-resistant bottoms and grip handles, tubs with body contour designs for stretch-out soaking, tubs with whirlpool for hydromassage, and numerous combination tub-shower configurations.

Cast iron and formed steel still are the most widely used materials for bathtub construction, but heavy-duty fiberglass-reinforced polyester is making dramatic inroads because of one-piece construction and crisp lines not possible with older materials. The plastic units are easy to maintain with liquid cleaner and are ideal for remodeling purposes because of their lighter weight.

Lavatories No other bathroom fixtures come in as many styles, sizes, and shapes as the lavatory. Because it is often surrounded by attractive light fixtures, the medicine cabinet, countertop, and vanity, the area it occupies generally becomes the focal point in the average bathroom.

With such a variety of choices available, it is possible to select lavatories that fit the needs of children as well as adults. Since the lavatory may be needed for washing garments, in addition to washing face and hands and shampooing, a small lavatory should be used only when lack of space is an overriding problem.

The most popular lavatory for new construction and remodeling is the self-rimming model that seals directly to countertops for neater, quicker installation and minimum maintenance. Still other models install directly on vanity cabinets with a metal ring or frame holding the unit in place, under tile, marble, or plastic laminate countertops.

Fixture installation standards for lavatories call for a minimum depth of 16 inches for the countertop extension from the wall surface, with the average counter in the 20-to 24-inch range. Twin lavatories should be installed with a minimum 16 inches from the center of one bowl to the center of the other bowl. Greater spacing is highly desirable when children are to use the fixtures.

Most lavatories used by adults are installed 34 to 38 inches from floor to top of the bowl. This dimension frequently is reduced to 31 inches when children 5 feet 2 inches or shorter are to use the fixture. Keep in mind that the initial height selected can be modified at a later date by adding a new cabinet and longer supply and drain lines. Mirrors and medicine cabinets should be a minimum of 8 inches above the countertop-bowl surface to minimize splashing problems.

This multipurpose lavatory for bedroom or bathroom is designed to expand as the child grows. Initially it can be used for a miniature bath, later for a teenage shampoo lavatory. The drop-in fixture measures 28 × 19 inches and has a roomy 23 × 14 inch sloping basin. Photo courtesy of Kohler

If enough space is available, the family bath can serve adults on one side and children on the other, as shown here. Folding doors are used to save valuable wall space, and the built-in lavatory-vanity unit on the children's side has a pullout step-drawer for the little one. Photo courtesy of Armstrong Cork Company

Toilets In selecting a toilet, keep in mind that all toilets are not alike. Some look better, some work better, and some offer more convenience features than others. Some save water, some offer off-the-floor mounting for easier cleaning, and some have low silhouettes and space-saving designs.

Most toilets are available with either round or elongated bowl rims. The elongated bowl (sometimes referred to as extended rim) is 2 inches longer from the front edge of the rim to the back of the toilet. This shape is recommended for children as being more sanitary and easier to keep clean.

Off-the-floor toilets require 2 × 6 support studding instead of the conventional 2 × 4 studs used in most home walls. This can be accomplished quite simply during new construction or for add-on rooms; however, it is more difficult to install in an existing wall.

Toilets should be installed with 1-inch clearance from the back wall, a minimum of 8 inches from a facing wall or cabinet, and a minimum of 15 inches from the center of the bowl to each side wall or cabinet. Keep in mind that replacing an outdated toilet is not a major undertaking. The existing plumbing will accommodate newer fixtures, and new water-supply lines are relatively inexpensive.

Fittings Plumbing fittings for a child's bathroom should be of the premixed type whenever possible. Handle and dial models that control both hot and cold water with a single hand are far easier for the young child to handle than are two-valve units with two handles. The single-control fitting enables control of water temperature by movement of the control to the right or left. The volume is controlled by moving the same control in and out, or backward and forward.

Two other wise investments in selecting bathroom fittings for children's use are pressure balancing and thermostatic controls. Volume on the pressure balancing valve is usually preset, and the valve maintains that temperature automatically, preventing scalds. This is accomplished by a pressure-sensing device that

automatically decreases the flow of either the hot or the cold water when the operating pressure in the opposite line drops. Should the pressure of the cold water supply drop sufficiently to cause scalding, the valve automatically shuts off the hot water flow. This pressure balancing valve is most commonly found controlling a shower head.

The thermostatic control employs a heat-sensing device to automatically adjust the hot and cold volume to maintain a preselected temperature of mixed water. This type of valve gives a more precise temperature than the pressure balancing valve, and it usually permits the user to control volume as well as temperature.

Shower Fittings Another bathroom fitting that is growing rapidly in popularity, particularly for use by children, is the personal shower that offers the bather the convenience of leaving the shower head in place in a wall-mount or detaching a flexible hose to hold the unit. Most major firms that manufacture personal showers offer products that give the bather a choice of two or three different sprays in the same head—sprays to massage, pound, or tingle.

The circus theme employed here helps encourage a child's acceptance of bathtime, while the fixtures are designed for both personal and room cleanliness. Among the desirable features for a child's bath are: splashproof tub enclosure with wall safety bar, bathtub with safety grab rails, vinyl flooring, plastic laminate countertop with removable safety bar for baby diapering, off-the-floor water closet, bidet, shampoo lavatory and storage areas within reach of a child. Photo courtesy of Kohler

Although personal showers are designed to replace a regular shower head, some manufacturers make a diverter valve to allow the choice of using the hand shower or the regular head. Diverter heads can also be used to outfit bathtub spouts with a hand shower operation.

Mounting accessories for personal showers include chrome-plated wall bars in 24 or 42-inch lengths to permit sliding the shower head up and down so that it can be positioned high for adults and low for small children. The hose length for most models is approximately 5 feet, but shorter or longer hoses are readily available.

Lighting

Proper lighting in the bathroom is just as important for children as for adults. There should be good overall lighting with specialized lighting in key areas. Balanced lighting on either side of the mirrors is ideal for teens as they enter the makeup/shaving phase of life.

There should be a light over the tub and in the shower. Most designers will strongly recommend the use of a combination light-ventilating fan in the shower to remove the steam before it fogs mirrors. Improvements in fluorescent lamps make them highly usable in the bathroom and equal to incandescent light, long known for providing true color for makeup.

Space permitting, medicine cabinets should not be placed directly over the lavatory. Installations to the side or in a corner provide better utility and allow large, well-illuminated mirror expanse. Additional lighting information can be found in a later chapter.

Storage

It is one thing to accessorize the children's bath and another to clutter. Cosmetics and such sundries should be concealed in nearby storage areas. Handy-height wood or chrome ladders are excellent for youngsters' towel storage. Face towels require an 18-inch bar per pair, with a hanging depth of 15 to 23 inches. Bath towels require a 24-inch per pair bar width, with a hanging depth of 20 to 24 inches. A commonly used rule-of-thumb allows 27 inches of rod space per person. Towel bars in most bathrooms are installed 36 to 42 inches off the floor. Cups, toothbrushes, and other commonly used bathroom items should be readily accessible to children.

Wallcoverings

Vinyls Vinyls are a good choice for the bathroom because they are washable, strippable, and have a relatively high resistance to the moisture that results from showers and baths. Because changes in heat and humidity can loosen wallcovering, it is important to hang the material properly. For paper-backed vinyl

Most home showers with their high shower heads can be easily adapted to child use with the installation of a hand-held shower. This three-spray unit quickly attaches to a wall shower arm or special tub spout to provide three different water flows—massage spray, soft aerated spray, or regular spray. Flexible hose length for most models is 59 inches, and other lengths are available on request. This type of unit has a wall mount that can be positioned at any height. Photo courtesy of Ondine

wallcovering, use a vinyl adhesive. For cloth-backed, use a mixture of part powdered vinyl adhesive plus part premixed. The use of a vinyl adhesive rather than a wheat paste will prevent mildew.

Ceramic Tiles Ceramic tile is probably the most popular material used for floors and walls in the bathroom. In addition to the traditional singly-applied tiles, there are now available sheet squares of tile applied to a backing that can be put up in blocks and the grout can be added between the tiles afterward.

Retreats — Attics, Basements, Studies

Parents are quick to recognize that preteens and teenagers have needs that are different from those of younger children. They are a separate kind of human being—neither child nor adult—and industries of every description are vying to supply their special needs. Parents are being urged to provide separate quarters for preteens and adolescents. Accordingly, this chapter presents alternatives that will satisfy the need for privacy, individualism, and peace and quiet. Retreats in the attic and basement are discussed, as well as study areas set apart as much as possible from everyday traffic.

Attics

Skylights The recent dramatic improvements in skylights have greatly expanded the possibilities of converting wasted attic space into additional living space. Where it was once necessary to build an expensive dormer into the roof to provide required natural light and ventilation, you now can cut a hole in the roof

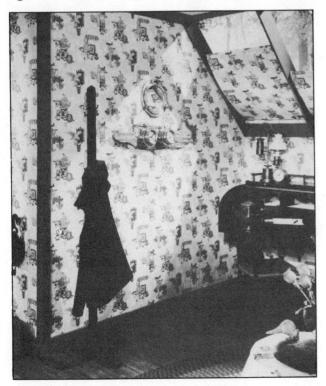

Opening up a section of the roof and closing it again with windows or skylights helps to make attic space more appropriate for children's rooms. The wallcovering and matching window shades depict the days of the clipper ships. Photo courtesy of Wallcovering Industry Bureau

and install a weatherproof, operable window.

Skylights today come in all shapes and sizes with clear or translucent glass or plastic, with most units offered in package form for simple homeowner installation. Most are double glazed to provide necessary insulation, and some are tinted to filter the sun and eliminate glare.

Manufacturers produce skylights to fit snugly between standard rafter spacing on 16, 32, and 48-inch centers. The needed opening is cut from inside the attic, and roofing materials are then removed and replaced according to the specific instructions provided with each particular style and brand. Direction of the natural light can be straight, angled, or flared depending upon the unit selected.

Conversion Considerations In most homes, the attic generally serves as a storage area for items placed there for future use. Many attics have full or partial subfloors; many are unheated. All attics should be insulated regardless of their use both to save energy and to make the balance of the home more comfortable for daily living.

More than any other room in the home, the attic best accommodates built-in furniture that conserves space and makes best use of low, sloping roof lines and short knee walls. Built-in beds, for example, can be placed along the short walls while the higher-ceiling center area of the room is better used for traffic movement. Likewise, extended dormer areas already in existence in many homes provide an excellent location for study desks built between flanking walls.

Many attic knee walls also hold the key to added organized storage gained through the simple installation of a plywood floor and access doors leading from the reclaimed room area.

To coordinate a room that is cut up spatially, such as converted attic space, use the same finishing material throughout. Fabric-backed vinyl wallcovering is strong enough to be used on many surfaces. You can apply it not only to walls but also to built-in fronts and even freestanding pieces, such as tables or cubed furniture.

Study Areas

The home study center, when well planned and well lighted, is a considerable asset that can be expected to pay lifetime dividends. Many youngsters find themselves faced with school homework or study each day,

Wasted attic space was remodeled into a teenager's retreat with fold-down hanging desk, wall-hung shelving, cabinets built under the sofa bed, and efficient lighting. The room is fully carpeted and has easy-to-maintain walls of 1×8-inch V-groove western wood paneling. Note below the desk that additional storage has been fitted into the lower part of the sloping walls. Photo courtesy of Western Wood Products Association

In supplying storage areas for children in the home, oftentimes a special-purpose area can be part of the scheme. Here an L-shaped loft was transformed into a library-study-game center. The built-in bookcases have adjustable shelves and a series of map drawers for art prints, maps, and the like. Walls of the stairwell are paneled with clear-finished hemlock for easy maintenance. Photo courtesy of Western Wood Products Association

with only an inadequate study location such as the kitchen table.

Lighting Needs General Electric's lighting experts have researched the proper home study center and report that home study involves the elements of concentration, a fixed position, and critical eye use—elements which must be properly correlated for the student if his studying is to be effective. The ease, comfort, efficiency, and accuracy with which the student's eyes perform are dependent upon the quality and quantity of lighting in his visual field and on the study task.

In planning a home study center, parents should strive to provide an area in which the student is relaxed and comfortable. Of major importance is a permanent, level work surface that is the student's own, always ready and equipped for his study needs. A desk or table with a surface of about 24 × 46 inches

gives sufficient working space. The surface should be nonreflective, and light in color. If the surface is dark, it should be covered with a pastel blotter or construction paper.

The desk should be positioned flat against a wall (never in front of a window) and away from family activity or conversation areas. If the wall is dark or boldly patterned, cover the area in front of the desk with light-colored tackboard or pegboard.

The desk surface should be 28 to 29 inches above the floor to accommodate an adjustable-posture chair seat that will raise the student and correctly locate his eye level in relation to the desk top. General Electric engineers recommend the eye position should be at least 14 inches above the work surface. Books and other reading matter should be propped or tilted about 30 degrees toward the eyes. If the book is flat on the work surface, the type is shortened and reading is more difficult.

A pair of lamps, either wall-hung or table-based, provide the best work lighting, since light comes from two directions to cover the whole desk top; however, most homes do not have a study desk large enough to accommodate a pair of table-based lamps. Decorative appropriateness for the desk and for the room must also be considered in deciding between a single lamp or a pair, or between wall-hung versus table-type lamps.

Because it is so close to the eye, a lamp shade that is dark in color or that transmits too great an amount of light can be a source of distraction and eye strain. The inside should be white, or nearly so, to reflect the light efficiently over the work area. An example of an inefficient study lamp is the popular two-globe Colonial lamp; it makes an attractive decoration, but puts too high a level of brightness right in the user's eyes.

Table-based lamps should measure 15 to 16 inches from table top to bottom edge of the shade. This assures the user's eyes will be nearly in line with the lower edge of the shade when he is in normal reading position.

Because study lamps are nearly always located close to and in front of the student's work and eyes, it is important that these lamps be equipped with diffusing bowls or discs to soften reflected glare. The shade should flare at the bottom for best distribution of light. Minimum diameters for shade bottoms are 16 inches

for a single table-based lamp, 15 inches for a single wall-hung lamp, and 10 inches for two wall-hung lamps when used as a pair.

Placement of the desk table lamp (or window) is best at the left side of a right-handed person. Wall-mounted scissor-bracket lamps are recommended for desks deeper than 24 inches, as these fixtures can be pulled out nearer the front edge of the desk when in use and pushed back against the wall when not in use.

While many "bullet" lamps have been sold for desk use, these fixtures have a major drawback in that they put a hot spot on the book being read, washing out the contrast of black print on white page and reducing visibility. This type of lamp, no matter how well placed, cannot provide full, even illumination on the study area.

Fluorescent lamps teamed with incandescent lamps can provide excellent light for a student study center. Lighting specialists suggest the fluorescent light source be no more than 12 inches back from the front edge of the desk or table to prevent reflection in the user's eyes. A 30-watt 36-inch deluxe warm white tube is minimum for most desks.

Other important components of a study center include convenient book storage, properly located convenience outlets for such items as radio, typewriter, and tape deck, and a source of fresh air.

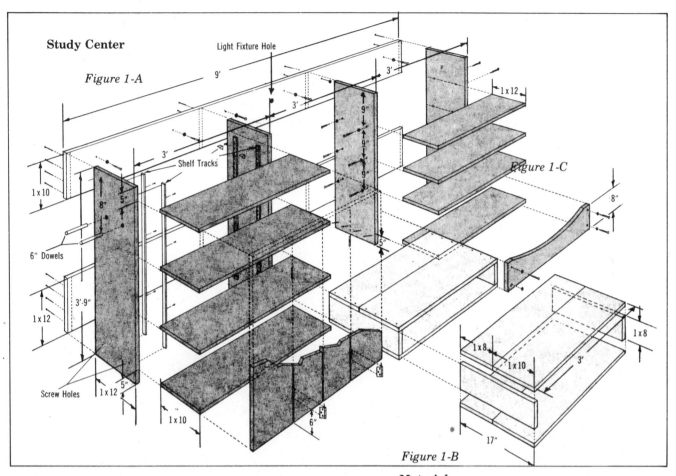

Study Center

Figure 1-A

Light Fixture Hole

9'

3'

3'

1 x 12

Shelf Tracks

9"

9"

9"

Figure 1-C

1 x 10

8"

5"

8"

6" Dowels

5"

3'-9"

1 x 12

Screw Holes

5"

1 x 12

1 x 10

1 x 8

1 x 8

1 x 10

3'

6"

6"

17"

Figure 1-B

Precut all pieces. Square ends.

*A: Predrill screw holes in upright dividers, placing holes 4¾"
from top and bottom edges. Drill two holes for coat hanger
dowels. Cut shelf tracks to 32" and screw onto dividers 6"
apart. (Figure 1-A) Construct unit with glue, screws, and
grommets.*

B: Glue and nail as per figure 1-B.

*C: Predrill screw holes in dividers as located in Figure 1-C.
Construct unit. Hint: when affixing permanent shelves, predrill screw holes ½" into end of shelf to prevent splitting.*

*When purchasing lumber, remember that actual widths and
depths are slightly less than stock measurements. A 1×10
stock board, for example, is actually ¾" × 9½".*

*It took less than a day to assemble the cabinet-shelf-desk
combination for a child's room (left). Pegs in the end wall
provide hanging storage, and the desk is topped with plastic laminate. Shelves at right are fixed in place while those
in the cabinet can be adjusted in height. Photo courtesy of
Western Wood Products Association*

Materials

Backboards:	1 piece 1" × 10" × 9'
	1 piece 1" × 12" × 9'
Upright Dividers:	4 pieces 1" × 12" × 3'-9"
Shelves:	4 pieces 1" × 10" × 2'-10½"
	4 pieces 1" × 12" × 2'-10½"
Doors:	2 pieces 1" × 10" × 3'
	2 pieces 1" × 8" × 3'
Bin Front:	1 piece 1" × 8" × 3'
Bin Bottom:	1 piece 1" × 12" × 2'-10½"
Desk Sides:	2 pieces 1" × 6" × 1'-5"
Desk Top:	1 piece 1" × 8" × 1'-5"
	1 piece 1" × 10" × 3'
Desk Bottom:	1 piece 1" × 8" × 3'
	1 piece 1" × 10" × 3'
Dowels:	2 pieces ¾" × 6"
Bulletin Board:	Cork or fiberboard 2' × 3'
Shelf Hardware:	4 pieces shelf standard 3'
	24 shelf supports
Door Hardware:	8 butt hinges 1½" × ¾"
	2 wood door pulls
	2 catches (friction or magnetic)
Screws and Grommets:	3 dozen No. 10 roundhead 1½" wood screws (bright finish)
	3 dozen bright finish grommets
Glue:	2 fluid ounces white glue
Toggles (if needed):	6 toggle bolts 2½"

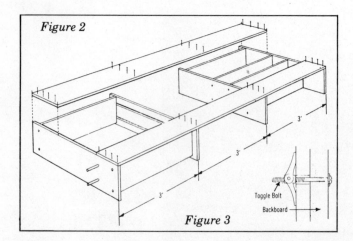

Figure 2

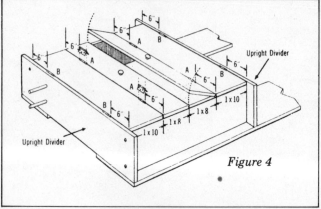

Figure 3

2. *Place units A and C face down on floor (Figure 2) gluing and nailing backboards flush across tops and bottoms. Be sure space allotted unit B is 3 feet.*

3. *Construct doors as shown in Figure 4, attaching A hinges where indicated. Measure and drill hinge B screw holes on dividers. Attach B hinges to doors. Do not attach doors to dividers until entire unit is mounted on wall.*

   To mount on wall, locate studs and drill backboard for screws or bolts. (To aid stud location, remember studs are generally placed on 16" centers.) If studs or other solid support are not available, use toggle bolts (Figure 3).

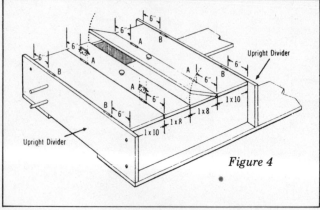

Figure 4

4. *Support unit to desired height and attach to wall. Recommended clearance from bottom of lower shelves to floor: children ages five to twelve, 18" to 24"; adults, 26" to 28".*

   Mount unit B by drilling, gluing, and screwing through sides of units A and C. Bottom of desk should be flush with bottom of A's lower shelf.

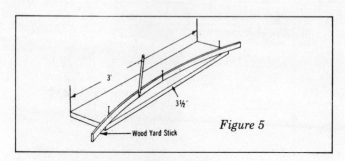

Figure 5

5. *Using a wooden yardstick, scribe an arc (Figure 5) and cut bin front with keyhole saw or jigsaw. Drill and attach with screws and grommets flush with bottom of desk (1-C).*

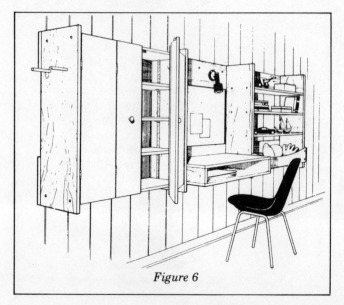

Figure 6

6. *Mount bulletin board on wall using screws and grommets or strong adhesives. Mount doors, pulls, and catches. Glue and insert dowel coat hangers. Install light and insert adjustable shelves. Finish as desired.*

Wood Paneling for a Study Wall Consider wood paneling for one wall of a teenager's room. The paneling is sound-absorbing, which is a decided advantage. It may also add resale value to your house.

To cover one wall and create a study center large enough for two, follow the instructions and photos on the following pages.

Steps:

1. *Determine lumber needed. Trim is measured by linear foot. Add to wall requirements sufficient baseboard molding for desk front. Add ceiling molding to finish back and sides of desk top and an equal amount to use as cleats to support desk top. To determine amount of lumber needed for paneling, determine the square footage of the walls and convert this to board and linear feet of lumber, using the conversion factors provided by the California Redwood Association.*

   First multiply each wall's total width by its height and subtract nonpaneled areas, windows, and doors. Then multiply this figure by the board and linear foot conversion factors appropriate for the width of your lumber. Paneling 100 square feet of wall space with 6-inch side lumber requires 115 board feet ($100 \times 1.15 = 115$) or 230 linear feet ($115 \times 2 = 230$). Be sure to allow 5 percent extra for errors and end trim loss.

2. *Store redwood lumber for several days away from moisture, direct sunlight, and heat vents, preferably in the room to be paneled.*

3. *Remove all outlet and switch plates (tape screws to each to avoid losing them), and hot and cold air duct covers. If you want to extend outlet boxes for added paneling thickness, shut off electricity at the fuse panel beforehand. Outlets also may be left neatly recessed. As individual boards go up, cut openings, measuring from the adjoining board and from the floor or ceiling. Mark dimensions in the panel face; drill four large holes just inside marked corners, and saw from them with a saber or keyhole saw.*

4. *Arrange lumber before you glue paneling, creating the most attractive variations from one board to next. Begin vertical paneling at an inside corner. Work left to right if you are right-handed, right to left if left-handed. Keep groove edges toward the starting corner, and tongue edges toward your work direction. Trial-fit the first board and check for plumb, then nail with 5d or 6d finishing nails, even if other boards are to be glued on.*

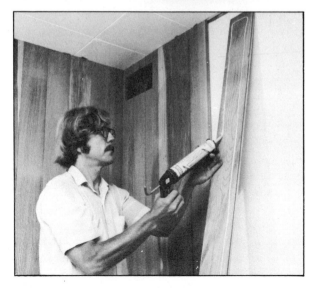

5. *Measure all other boards carefully and trial-fit. Tap them into place with a hammer and tapping block, a scrap with the groove edge intact to fit over board tongues. Check for plumb, and, if necessary, slightly angle groove-to-groove fitting to make it square. When butt-joining short board ends together in the middle of a wall, be sure the joint falls over a stud, blocking, or furring strip.*

6. *To glue panels, apply adhesive generously with caulking gun to the back of a prefitted board. Let it set according to adhesive package directions, then hold the board to the wall so both are coated. Remove it, wait again, then tap the board into place, and face-nail top and bottom with 8d finishing nails (two nails at each end for wider boards). During waiting periods, you can finish one board while adhesive sets on another.*

7. *The last board may have to be trimmed to fit into a corner. Angle trim the board's corner edge slightly with a block plane, with the wide part of the angle toward the wall.*

8. *To install redwood moldings and baseboards, measure floors and ceilings separately. Miter join molding and baseboard ends on outside corners, and butt-join them on inside corners.*

9. *Finish wall as desired.*

10. *To make study area, use plastic laminated desk top or, if the area is small enough, a flush door; install shelf brackets and redwood planks for use as shelving. NOTE: You can use single-groove fascia for shelving and allow the bracket front end to fit into the groove so the bracket heads do not show. This results in the free-floating effect of the shelving in the illustration.*

11. *Set desk top at 26-inch height for greatest comfort. Nail ceiling molding around sides and back where desk will be attached underneath as a support. Use L brackets to attach legs made from redwood plank or fascia to desk top from underneath. Nail desk top to supporting molding cleats.*

12. *Finish desk top by nailing on ceiling molding around back edge and sides, into wall instead of desk top. Finish front edge with baseboard molding, flush with desk top and overhanging below desk. Finish desk and shelving redwood to match wall finish.*

Basements

Homeowners with children have found the basement an excellent place to gain valuable living area at minimum cost, often doubling the usable floor area of a home. Depending upon the age of the children who will use this space, the basement can literally grow with the youngsters as they progress from building blocks to teenage parties.

To many, the basement has long been a storage area for a lot of things that worked their way from frequent to infrequent usage. Often this ready-to-improve space has been plagued with dampness, poor lighting, and total lack of decoration.

Preplanning your basement space for children's use need not be complicated or overly elaborate. Begin with a floor plan that sectionalizes the total area according to the specific uses you desire. Frequently these will include separate spaces for heating and storage, laundry, workshop, game room, TV room, and recreation or playroom.

Combating Excess Moisture Assuming that you will want to use these spaces all year, you must initially handle the problem of summer condensation of moisture from the air. This problem occurs when warm, moist air from the outdoors comes in contact with cool basement walls and floors, and with uninsulated cold water pipes. The water then condenses on the cool surfaces. Dampness caused by condensation can usually be cured by warming the basement through either ventilation, insulation, or extension of heating, or by reduction in the amount of moisture in the basement by dehumidifying. By opening basement windows in dry weather, the walls and floors can be warmed in the summer. An exhaust fan installed in a basement window and operated during the day is helpful in circulating air through the basement. Ventilation alone, however, is not a very dependable cure for moisture problems. Waterproofing paint can be part of your solution, although it is frequently not sufficient in itself.

The amount of moisture in a basement can be reduced by a mechanical dehumidifier which extracts the moisture and deposits it in a tank or allows it to run down the drain. The mechanical dehumidifier is essentially a small refrigeration unit, and the moisture in the air condenses on the coils since they are colder than any other surface in the basement. Some heat is given off in the operation of a dehumidifier which further helps to control condensation.

Walls can be kept above the temperature of the ground by the use of insulation. When the walls are warmer, the moisture in the air will not condense readily on them. Moisture-resistant insulation and a

Before remodeling, this unfinished basement was the junk-yard for a typical family's paraphernalia. With careful planning and do-it-yourself enthusiasm, it evolved into a cozy, versatile space suitable for a variety of activities by all members of the family.

By building a boxed beam and enclosing a steel post, an attractive dining nook was created. The breakfast/snack bar is delineated with fluorescent lighting integrated in the suspended acoustical ceiling and hides overhead pipes and ducts. Walls are covered with paneling concealing fuse boxes and plumbing. Photo courtesy Armstrong Cork Company

built-in vapor barrier must be used. To reduce the amount of water that collects on cold water pipes, insulate them with foamed or wrapped insulation.

Decorative Possibilities

Whitewash no longer is the standard decor for basements. Pastel colors are available in long-lasting portland cement base paints that can provide many decorative schemes. In addition, hundreds of different prefinished wood and hardwood panelings are available from local retail lumber dealers for use in the basement.

Partitions Walls dividing basements into specific use areas need not be load-bearing in design and thus are easier for the homeowner to construct. Such partitions are easily attached to concrete floor surfaces with power stud drivers, while top plates are simply nailed to the overhead floor joist. Electrical wiring can be easily strung in the overhead areas and along studs of the new partitions to provide convenient outlets and wall switches.

Sound Control Sound conditioning is an important phase of construction in creating basement space for children. The two key areas, of course, being floor and ceiling.

Do-it-yourself materials on the market make it a relatively easy job to install a suspended acoustical ceiling that will reduce noise levels and hide unsightly pipes and ducts. Such ceilings with a metal grid system and "lay in" panels frequently are designed to also accommodate luminous ceiling lighting panels that eliminate the need for hanging fixtures.

Floors Basement floors (below grade) may be covered with special grades of resilient flooring, carpeting, and wood-finish flooring. Uneven floors can be made level by using 2 × 4 inch sleepers and shims to create a totally new floor surface.

Windows Most basements are constructed with small, hopper-style windows that open from the top and have an all-glass area of approximately 7 feet above the floor level. Such windows frequently are totally out of scale with finished-room decorating schemes and thus require special treatment to visually put them in scale. Small, high windows can be hidden with decorative blinds or window coverings that give the appearance of shielding full-size windows. Curtains that extend beyond each side or that fall below the bottom edge of the window will give this illusion. Generally speaking, these windows rarely need to be opened and therefore can be treated as

Accommodating a standard-size fold-up table-tennis table, an open area at one end of the basement also holds a pegboard storage wall with overhead fluorescent illumination. The vinyl flooring has a cushion back for comfort. Photo courtesy Armstrong Cork Company

totally fixed windows.

You might also consider creating false window fronts. Artificial windows can be built in with backlighting and an opaque sheet that diffuses light to simulate sunlight. For the best results, such windows should be installed in paneled walls with sufficient depth to accommodate an artificial window. Semi-transparent curtains or shutters will allow just a hint of the artificial sunlight to shine in.

For more detailed instructions on finishing off unused areas of the home, see *Finishing Off Additional Rooms*.

Storage

"A place for everything and everything in its place" may be an old saying, but it is nearly impossible to accomplish when it comes to a child's room.

Closets

The room's closet is an important storage facility for a child, yet it is always planned and built for adult use. How you change this storage will greatly affect what is out of place at the end of the day or after a thorough room cleaning.

The first change to make in the closet is to put at least one bar at the child's height. Since most children do not have an exceptionally large seasonal wardrobe, part of the width of the closet at this lower level can be fitted with removable box-style compartments into which shoes, toys, games, and other items can be placed by the youngster. The original closet bar can be retained for out-of-season clothing, or the bar simply removed and more cubicle and shelf space provided with a box added as a step to reach this area.

In addition to the bedroom closet, storage space for children's belongings can be located in other areas of the house.

Bedroom Storage Space under the bed can provide adequate easily accessible storage. Use low-height boxes, a plywood panel on casters, drawers, or small boxes to store infrequently used items.

The headboard is another location for additional storage space. Many beds come with compartments that can be used for book and other storage. Some headboards also have shelf-type tops that can be used for the radio, clock, and lamp.

The area around the headboard can be customized in a number of arrangements to make a working storage wall.

A chain or rope can be used to suspend various-sized baskets from the ceiling for very accessible storage of often used items.

The inside surface of swinging closet doors is often

Built-in redwood shelves and cabinets are attached to a wall of 1 × 6 redwood Clear All-Heart paneling. The raised bed platform simplifies vacuuming and has a convenient headboard divider for a tuner, a turntable, record storage, and a telephone. Photo courtesy of California Redwood Association

Dial-A-Closet fittings, produced by Wessel Hardware Corporation and sold throughout the country by local hardware and lumber dealers, permit you to increase hanging space in a closet by more than 50 percent and more than double the existing shelf space. Combinations of the various components fit any closet ranging from 29 to 121 inches wide.

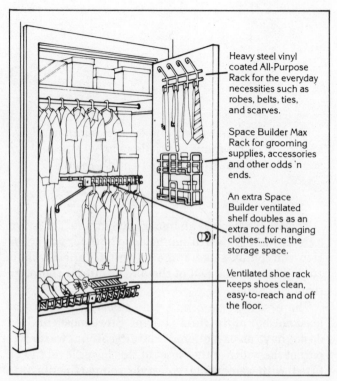

Heavy steel vinyl coated All-Purpose Rack for the everyday necessities such as robes, belts, ties, and scarves.

Space Builder Max Rack for grooming supplies, accessories and other odds 'n ends.

An extra Space Builder ventilated shelf doubles as an extra rod for hanging clothes...twice the storage space.

Ventilated shoe rack keeps shoes clean, easy-to-reach and off the floor.

Closet space can accommodate twice the usual contents when arranged in orderly fashion. This drawing shows ventilated shelving made of vinyl-coated steel rods. Drawing courtesy of Space Builder

used for tie racks in an adult bedroom, but the same space can be used for any number of child items. Small boxes and shelves with rails prove most handy.

That old college trunk or army footlocker placed at the foot of the bed provides closed storage for toys, games, and other childhood treasures.

Divider walls can be another excellent source of additional storage. When used to create separate sleeping areas for two or more youngsters, these partitions can be equipped with drawers and shelves.

Bathroom Storage Most bath specialty stores offer a selection of floor-to-ceiling storage units that can be quickly installed around a toilet and used for bath items. Still other units are designed for hanging on the wall directly over the toilet tank to make use of this otherwise wasted space.

If you are selecting a new bathtub, consider one that has an integral shelf for bath soaps, cosmetics, and water toys.

Wall-hung lavatories are the least expensive bathroom fixtures but have become less desirable with the widespread use of vanities that provide floor-to-bowl storage space. Towels, cleaning supplies, and toiletries can be neatly stored in a vanity.

Wood, plastic, and aluminum frame hanging shelf units available at many department stores or building

centers can be suspended on the outside of sliding bathtub-shower doors or on the end wall opposite bathtub faucets. Triangular corner shelves also require little space in a bathroom and yet permit open storage of much-used items such as bath salts, bubble bath, and soap. Additional bathroom storage ideas and projects can be found in *Bathroom Planning and Remodeling*.

General Storage Many newer homes built with window seats are framed in such a way that removal of facing wallboard provides a new under-window storage area. Window seats also provide small children with an opportunity to look out windows that may otherwise be out of reach.

Narrow-depth shelf storage can generally be installed between studs once the wall surfacing has been removed. Such areas in unfinished garages are good locations for storing baseball bats, skis, archery sets, and other narrow toys or sporting equipment.

Some builders provide storage area beneath the stairways, but in homes where they do not, removal of wallboard and installation of access doors provide excellent storage for a child's use.

Space on either side of a wall usually can be converted to a storage-style room divider, with shelf and cabinet space designed specifically for your storage needs including stereo equipment, tape decks, record

This children's bedroom incorporates a western motif. The Indian tipi provides an excellent creative play environment for the child. Photo courtesy of Masonite

This well-designed bedroom for two children (left) features a linen canvas tent complete with two folding surplus army cots, folding mattresses, and down comforters. The painted steel shelving is completely adjustable. Notice the matching canvas window shades. Photo courtesy of Belgian Linen Association

The seaworthy room (right) combines easy-care carpeting, self-stick floor tiles, a wood plank ceiling, and new furniture in a marine motif. A child's interests should always be included in the design. Photo courtesy of Armstrong Cork Company

This bedroom-playroom combination features separate sleep, storage, play and study areas. The room was designed to permit one child to sleep without being disturbed by another child working at the desk. Photo courtesy of Armstrong Cork Company

Open cabinets can accommodate a child's interests at any age. Notice the matching quilt pattern of the wallpaper and draperies. A deep pile carpeting was added to provide a warmer floor surface. Photo courtesy of Albert Van Luit

All of the furniture in this girl's room (right) was constructed by the homeowner. A dark wallpaper contrasts well with the light furniture and accents. Photo courtesy of Armstrong Cork Company

In this little girl's room, the beds were recessed in a space created by building the two closets that flank the window. Photo courtesy of Armstrong Cork Company

Children's storage can be provided in a variety of beautiful and interesting ways. Here simple wicker bicycle baskets are suspended from a decorative drapery rod. A larger wicker basket serves as a footlocker. Photo courtesy of Armstrong Cork Company

The divider shelves (right) provide a separate area for each child in this colorful bedroom. The desk and shelving on the opposite wall were easily constructed of plywood. Photo courtesy of American Plywood Association

An excellent way to decorate a child's room is to incorporate some of the child's art. Photo courtesy of Masonite

A creative playroom (left) includes play equipment, a study area, and bright cheerful colors. Such a room can be constructed of framing and plywood. Photo courtesy of Champion Building Products

A bedroom-play area should incorporate the child's primary interests in a well-designed, open environment. Here (above) vinyl floor covering also provides easy maintenance. Photo courtesy of Armstrong Cork Company

There are several floor covering materials available on which games can be played. Note the use of nets as storage containers at the foot of the twin beds (right). Photo courtesy of Armstrong Cork Company

Homemade furniture has many advantages such as money savings, custom dimensions and designs that reflect a child's interests. Photo courtesy of Armstrong Cork Company

This storage unit-study area provides storage for clothes, books, toys, and sports equipment. The wall unit, desk, and chair were all constructed of wood and achieve a good balance of open and hidden storage. Photo courtesy of Western Wood Products

This attic (left) was converted into a spacious bedroom-play area for two children. The study-sleep area has a large open area in the center of the room for play activities.

A small room can be furnished to maximize the use of space (lower left). The lower bed fits beneath the upper bed to conserve space and provide more play area. Photo courtesy of American Plywood Association

A cedar storage wall was constructed at one end of this room (right). The unit provides shelves, drawers, and closet space to completely organize all of the child's belongings. Photo courtesy of Western Wood Products

Simple storage can be provided by placing a sturdy piece of wood on top of two file cabinets (left) or by building a bunk bed above storage drawers (below). Photo at left courtesy of American Plywood Association, photo below courtesy of Western Wood Products

This easy-to-build work space unit (left) folds out of a standard closet to provide a sturdy, uncluttered area for work or play. Plans for this project are available from the American Plywood Association.

Well-planned built-ins can help eliminate clutter in a child's room. This open-shelf unit (below) provides desk space and ample shelving. Photo courtesy of Western Wood Products

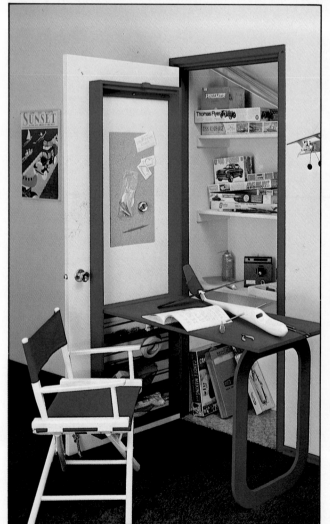

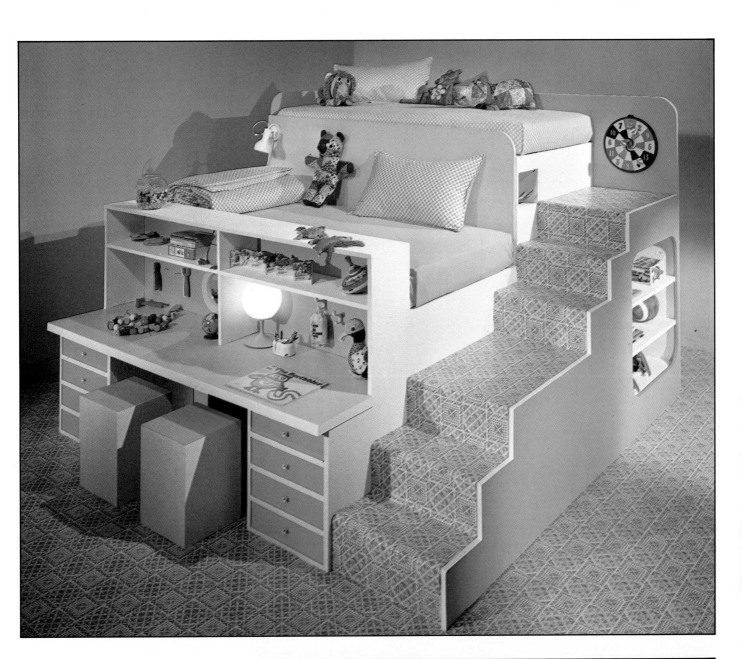

This total environment unit for two children can be built with plywood. The unit includes desk, drawers, shelves, a long storage area under the stairs, and two bunk beds. Photo courtesy of GAF

Many older homes do not have ample closet space. This complete bunk bed unit acts as bunk beds, closet, and dresser. The steps to the top bunk can also be used for storage. Photo courtesy of the American Plywood Association

The finished climbing structure is ideal for hard physical play. The structure helps children develop basic physical skills and coordination and can easily withstand a crowd of neighborhood children.

After the framework for one side has been assembled, the short posts for the railing and the railing boards should be assembled carefully with screws. Sturdy fastening ensures safety and durability.

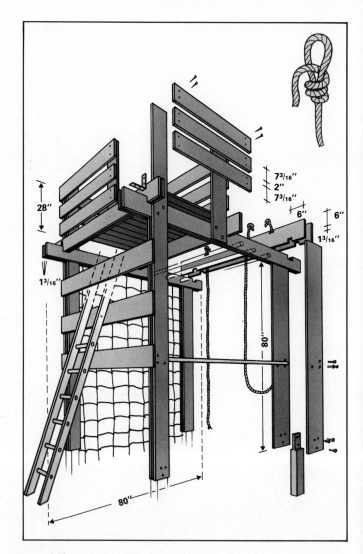

Building a Backyard Jungle Gym

It is important for children to develop the physical skills and coordination that will be needed to perform many daily activities. The jungle gym shown on these two pages will aid in this development. The gym offers a variety of climbing tasks: on netting, ropes, and a ladder. Children can also swing, hang, pull up, and engage in creative play. The jungle gym can be easily constructed from materials available at most lumber-supply stores.

The structure can be built of standard 2 x 6 or 2 x 8 lumber. If treated lumber is available, use it. Lumber either treated with pentachlorophenol (PCP) or Wolmanized is satisfactory. Creosoted material is not; it will dirty clothing. Even if you do not use treated material for the superstructure, it is important to use it for the foundation pieces.

Within a few hours, the entire structure can be prepared for construction.

Preliminary Work The foundation posts should be about 36 inches long, notched to receive the uprights about 10 inches from the end. Use either 4 x 6s or 4 x 8s for these, depending on what you are using for the superstructure.

The eight pieces holding the verticals together, as

Assembly begins with the posts which are to be set into the ground. A tenon should be cut at one end to which the two verticals are attached with threaded bolts and nuts. The tenon should be the same thickness as the vertical member.

This is the joint for the parallel beams. The vertical members are screwed to the horizontal boards in a type of sandwich construction. The parallel beam is fastened with an angle bracket attached with screws.

The floorboards are securely nailed to the crossboard and the outer parallel rail (lower right). Countersink all nails to prevent injury.

Stability is essential. To give the structure added support, place rocks into the hole around the post. Fill the hole with dirt or sand and water. After a few minutes, tamp thoroughly and repeat if necessary.

To prevent the climbing rope and swing from sliding, saw a notch into the parallel boards to hold the knot. Nail a piece of scrap lumber between the knots of the swing rope to prevent it from pulling out.

MATERIALS

Use 2 x 6s or 2 x 8s unless otherwise indicated.	**Ladder** 2 2 x 4s, 106½″ 11 hardwood dowels for rungs 1 x 16″
Vertical Posts 6 8′0″, cut to 86″ 2 10′0″, cut to 118″	**Miscellaneous** 4 foundation posts 4 x 6s or 4 x 8s, 36″
Horizontal Ring Beams 9 8′0″, cut to 79″	3 climbing boards, 70″ 1 horizontal bar, 60″
Commando Tower 3 pieces 40″ 3 pieces 72″ 3 1 x 6s or 1 x 8s, 50″ 1″ floorboards about 32¼″ long to cover 67″	1″ hardwood dowel or pipe 3 horizontal bars, 6′6″ 26 feet of ¾″ rope 1 soccer net about 4′8″ x 7′3″ 4 framing clips Bolts, nails, screws, and glue

ring beams, are notched 1¼ inches deep by 4½ inches wide to receive lumber (check lumber thickness), 6 inches from the ends. Drill the four pieces for the horizontal bars. Drill through the two inside pieces and halfway through the outer members. These pieces also need to be notched for the piece that carries one end of the floorboards. These members are attached by lag screws between and inside the verticals.

The other four are bolted together with blocking in between to form two crossbeams.

Into the ladder sides drill 1 inch holes 8 inches apart. Cut small wedges out of the ends of the rungs, about 1½ inches long, to form notches. Glue and nail the rungs into position and then drive somewhat larger wedges into the notches to lock the rungs into position.

If you are using untreated lumber, you may wish to brush on two coats of preservative at this point.

Construction Connect the verticals to the foundation pieces, which are set about 24 inches into the ground. Of course, make sure that the foundation posts are level with each other.

At 6 foot 6 inch height, attach the horizontal ring beams with lag screws. The notches must be to the outside of the vertical pieces (see drawing).

The short posts for the railing and the railing itself are attached with screws. Assemble the other side the same way.

Use metal framing clips to attach the ring beams to each other. Screw or nail floorboards to the beams. Reinforce the post at the left of the railing with a piece of scrap lumber.

Fold net at the edges over strips which are inserted between verticals and secured with screws. Attach lower horizontal bar with three carriage bolts at each end. Protruding ends of the bolts should be sawed off and filed smooth for safety.

The rope ends should have double knots (see drawing). Pull the rope end through the loop and tighten.

The ladder is stuck into the ground and fastened at the top to the protruding end of the ring beam with three screws.

Finish by fastening the three horizontal boards on the ladder side with screws.

Playhouse design is only limited by budget and imagination. This two-story unit provides a private area in which children may play and learn. Photo courtesy of Western Wood Products

Modular furniture available for children's rooms presents countless ways in which convenient storage can be assembled and then changed as needs change. This arrangement in- *corporates a platform bed and prefabricated storage units. Photo courtesy of Syroco*

storage, TV, and books. Plans for constructing these units are offered by most building material dealers.

Kitchen cabinet units offered in most major lines include special cabinets for corner use, either as wall or base style. These kitchen cabinet units are no longer restricted to the kitchen. They are appropriate for dens, dining areas or practically any room where additional storage is needed.

The book, *Space Saving Shelves and Built-ins* offers several plans and ideas for adding storage to the home.

A small-space bedroom for a teenager or college student can still offer order with a minimum cash outlay. This tiny room has wall-hung desk with pedestal drawer units and an open ledge to hold all paper supplies. The room is paneled with flush-joint western hemlock boards finished clear. Shelves are adjustable, the bottom one equipped with fluorescent lighting strips. Woven-wood blinds fit within the window frames. Photo courtesy of Western Wood Products Association

Noise Control and Lighting

Sound Systems

Most parents are interested in having their children develop an appreciation of music, and thus expose them to quality music at an early age.

Telling someone what to purchase in high fidelity stereo equipment is like picking out a suit for someone else—there is an excellent chance it won't fit; it will be the wrong color or style, and it will remain in the closet. Teenagers especially should have the opportunity to select the music system that pleases their ears, if not yours.

Most young children begin their music enjoyment with a simple phonograph. They merely plug it into the wall and plop a record in place, with only the sound volume knob as a control. This is soon replaced with perhaps a clock-radio offering AM-FM bands. Then comes the stereo system, and the adult need for ear-plugs.

Acquisition of a stereo system, whether it is a set that is a single unit or series of matched components, depends on proper electronic ingredients, wisely selected and skillfully balanced. The purchase also depends on the ear and budget of the buyer.

In buying, be prepared to exercise the most sensitive judgment, particularly if one has an untrained or easily satisfied ear. For as one's ear grows in sensitivity, the stereo set acquired at an early stage may become less than satisfying.

Learn to listen for the varying characteristics of loudspeakers, for example. They reflect an almost human diversity—some are mellow, others brilliant in tone. There is excitement, no doubt, in the sheer volume of sound, even in noise. Hence careless listeners fall for the temptation of a loud system that relies mainly on the bass for its sound.

Before you buy, sample the sounds and check your taste against your budget. You can acquire a system as a package unit or through the use of components. The package variety is usually a radio-phonograph-tape deck combination sold in consoles.

Components are separate building blocks of a high-fidelity sound system, the basic components of which are a turntable, amplifier, and loudspeaker. You can add a radio tuner, tape recorder-player, and additional speakers for stereo arrangement. Usually each component is made by a different manufacturer. Components have several advantages.

- They fit easily into any room or decor and can be either permanently built in or put into anything from a bookcase to a table—or can be placed in specially built cabinets.
- Component systems can be assembled step by step. You don't have to buy them all at once. You can start with the essentials and add other units later. Also, your system can be upgraded piece by piece.

A basic understanding of high fidelity stereo is most important in making your selections. The first link of the system is a record changer or separate turntable and arm. It rotates a record and brings it in contact with the cartridge, a small sensitive device that traces the sound vibrations engraved in the record, converting them to electrical signals.

The second link, the amplifier, is the nerve center of your music system. It receives the tiny electrical impulses from a phono cartridge, radio tuner, or tape recorder and amplifies them until they are strong enough to drive a high fidelity loudspeaker system. Amplifiers are sometimes divided into two parts: the preamplifier containing all the controls and the power amplifier which produces the loudspeaker driving power from the signal supplied by the preamplifier.

The final link is the loudspeaker, which converts electrical signals from the amplifier back into the audible sound vibrations and projects the sound into the room.

In selecting a home music system it is well to have at least a general knowledge of the differences involved in high fidelity, stereo, and stereo quadraphonic. High-fidelity refers to the quality of reproduction. Stereophonic and stereo quadraphonic are methods. Actually, stereo may be high or low fidelity.

High Fidelity Designed to reproduce music free of distortion and outside noise, high fidelity endeavors to present every note and its overtones in exactly the same form, intensity, and character as its live counterpart.

Stereo Two dimensional, it arises from the fact that our ears receive sound waves from two sides. Sound is heard by one ear a little later than the other, with slightly different intensity and phasing. With monophonic sound, in which music comes from one loudspeaker, dimensional characteristics are lost. For stereophonic sound, music is recorded by two microphones placed a few feet apart. Sound from each microphone is transcribed separately. Each track or channel is reproduced separately but simultaneously and projected through two speakers. This permits us to hear the dimension of music, such as the width of a symphony orchestra, the depth of a stage, the individual placement and movement of soloists.

Stereo Quadraphonic This fairly recent innovation provides full, richer concert-hall sound by using all four channels of stereo records, tape recordings and special radio presentations.

Most stereo buffs and experts will tell you that you get exactly what you pay for when it comes to selecting equipment. It is always wise to buy the best equipment you can afford and to be certain that you will be able to add to the unit so you can upgrade with components that are compatible with your original purchases.

Acoustical Ceiling Tiles

If ever a product was invented with children in mind, it has to be acoustical ceiling material. The use of acoustical material on the ceilings of children's rooms greatly reduces the noise parents hear.

Home noise increases each year: stereo units become more powerful; more appliances are used; air conditioners are added. The eardrums of parents take a constant pounding.

Psychologists have found that it is not always the volume and variety of noises that can heighten nervous tension, but rather the frame of mind of the listener. It appears that while people who work around loud and predictable noises grow accustomed to them, people expect peace and quiet at home.

Use of carpets and drapes and correct placement of furniture can also help to insulate your home from outside noise and cut down some of the acoustical distractions of an active family. One of the biggest causes of noisy interiors is a smooth, hard ceiling that causes sound waves to bounce back into the room. A large percentage of sound waves from a stereo speaker, for example, bounce off ceilings just fractions of a second after the listener hears the direct waves. This causes a boom effect which not only detracts from the quality of the recorded sound but also can be annoying to family members in other rooms.

A ceiling covered with acoustical material can absorb up to 70 percent of the sound striking it. You can choose from materials that are affixed directly to the ceiling surface or suspended units that give a dropped ceiling effect.

Acoustical and decorative ceiling tiles have im-

proved dramatically from a visual standpoint. Units with precisely squared edges on all four sides fit snugly against one another to form a continuous unbroken surface. The manufacturing process permits highly sophisticated embossing on the tile face with appealing designs.

Installation of tile ceilings has been simplified to the point where almost any homeowner can handle the job with common household tools. Armstrong's Intergrid system, for example, eliminates cutting and nailing of wood furring strips and does not require stapling. Lightweight channels (or runners) are simply attached (or hung) from the existing ceiling, and the tiles are held in place with supporting cross tees which snap into place. The supporting gridwork then is completely hidden from view in the finished ceiling.

The Intergrid system accommodates either 12 × 12-inch tiles or larger 1 × 4-foot units and requires a 2-inch drop from the existing ceiling. A recessed fluorescent light fixture is also offered with the system, or the system also can be used with conventional hanging light fixtures.

Lighting

No room, for child or adult, can be properly planned and decorated without considering proper lighting. Just as air conditioning provides year-round comfort, adequate lighting adds to visual comfort and provides flexibility for various activities.

Adequate Lighting Lighting actually exists before a fixture is installed, for every surface reflects some of the natural light it receives. Light can be absorbed by dark surfaces or reflected by light surfaces and utilized as useful illumination.

General Electric lighting specialists stress that proper lighting begins with recommended reflectances for major surfaces. Ceilings should be pale color tints that reflect a minimum 60 percent to a maximum 90 percent; walls should be medium shades that reflect from 35 to 60 percent; and floors of carpeting, tile, or wood should reflect from 15 to 35 percent.

The reflectance levels of these major surfaces and the amount of light they receive form the backgrounds against which most visual activity takes place. They are always, whether we are aware of them or not, somewhere within our field of view. As a consequence our visual comfort, mental attitude, and emotional mood is influenced by the balance that exists between the sources of illumination, the items to be seen, and the backgrounds against which they are viewed.

Research has proven that modern home living requires three basic types of illumination; general or fill-in lighting of 5 to 10 footcandles; local or functional lighting for specific visual tasks; and accent or

General lighting in a child's bedroom is provided here by a fluorescent bracket above the closet doors. The unit contains two 40-watt warm-white tubes which are shielded on the bottom by a diffuser. The general lighting provides 5 to 10 footcandles throughout the room and 10 footcandles at the closet.

decorative lighting. Of these three, by far the most important is specific task lighting, which may range from a minimum 10 footcandles for card games to 200 footcandles for hobbies with small details.

With the wealth of data readily available to builders, architects, interior designers, and homeowners alike, there is no excuse today for inadequate lighting. Today's fixtures are both decorative and functional. They are related to the space, integrated with the furnishings, and can be planned to serve changing activity.

Selection Ceiling lighting fixtures may be surface-mounted, pendant, or recessed. Wall units can be placed in a cornice for downlighting only, used as valance lighting both upward and downward, or mounted on the wall surface for both upward and downward lighting. Portable lamps can provide light over an area 40 to 50 feet, with about five portable units required for an average-sized room if it is lighted exclusively by this method.

The lighted canopy above the mirror contains two 40-watt warm-white fluorescent lamps, channel-mounted to the ceiling and centered over the diffuser. The lighted canopy in the tub area has one 40-watt warm-white fluorescent tube. Total bath lighting is 182 watts, an energy-saving feature. Photo courtesy of General Electric

Two teenage girls share this bathroom which has twin lavatories and a lighted soffit—an efficient means of lighting at the mirror and general room lighting. Two rows of 40-watt warm-white fluorescents are used, along with three 50R20 bulbs located elsewhere in the room. Photo courtesy of General Electric

Lighting is a key decorating tool in this basement. The relaxation area has a recessed downlight that highlights the round table while three adjustable eyeball fixtures, on a dimmer, are aimed to light the music rack of the antique piano and wall behind. The adjacent area is used for dancing and has a series of downlights containing pink and blue-white reflector lamps that are on a dimmer for flexibility of lighting level. Photo courtesy of General Electric

Room Requirements With children uppermost in mind, here is a brief rundown on lighting for specific areas of the home:

- *Bedrooms*—These areas require general lighting with a three to five-socket ceiling-mounted or suspended fixture providing a total 150-200 watts; you can increase the fixture size in rooms over 150 square feet to provide 200 to 300 watts. If structural lighting is desired instead of a ceiling unit, provide 8 to 12 footcandles of illumination via a valance, cornice, or wall bracket. If a recessed unit is selected, two 40-watt fluorescent lamps should be used.

- *Bathrooms*—Lighting at the mirror will illuminate the average-sized bathroom. Compartmented areas will require additional localized lighting. For small mirrors, use a set of three fixtures (one above and one on each side) wired to one switch. Each fixture should be shielded with wall brackets centered 30 inches apart, 60 inches above the floor. The ceiling unit (a minimum of 12 inches in diameter) should be centered over the front edge of the washbowl or counter with two 60-watt bulbs or two to four 20-watt, 24-inch long fluorescent tubes. Large mirrors (36 inches or more in

width) should have a double row of recessed, deluxe warm-white 30-watt, 36-inch long or 40-watt, 48-inch long fluorescent tubes. Recommended soffit dimensions are 16 inches front to back, 8 inches deep, and the full length of counter. Mirrors also may be illuminated by theatrical-type units with exposed-lamp fixtures across the top and sides of the mirror, four to six 15-watt or 25-watt bulbs per strip. Separate compartments should have a minimum 75-watt R-30 recessed fixture, or 8-inch diameter 100-watt surface-mounted fixture or wall bracket. Showers and closed-in tubs should be illuminated with a recessed vaporproof fixture for a 75 or 100-watt bulb with the switch outside of the shower area. A 15-watt night-light also is recommended.

- *Study Desk Area*—Because of the great attention that should be given to this lighting function, this specific child center is covered in greater depth in the previous chapter.

- *Game and Hobby Areas*—Permanent game tables should be illuminated with four 75-watt R-30 floodlights recessed or surface mounted, with fixtures placed 2 feet out diagonally from each corner of the table. Ping-pong tables should have two surface-mounted, well-shielded 30-watt or two 40-watt fluorescent fixtures at each end of the table. Pool tables should have a recessed 150-watt, R-40 reflector floodlight centered over each half of the table. For carpentry or handicraft at a workbench, use an industrial reflector-type fixture with a minimum of two 40-watt cool-white fluorescent tubes for a 6-foot bench or a pair of 150-watt silvered-bowl bulbs in reflectors spaced 3 feet apart. Placement should be over the front edge of the bench.

General Reading Requirements Lighting engineers have established minimum standards for table, wall, and floor lamps for reading use. It should be remembered, however, that general illumination is a must in main areas used by children, for it appears most of their reading is done on the floor. Use of a table lamp for sit-down reading varies with the height of the table plus the lamp base height, but the major factor is keeping the 16 to 18-inch shade bottom approximately 40 inches from the floor and at eye level of the user. The bulb should be a three-way 50/250 or 100/300-watt or a soft-white 150, 200 or 50/150-watt. Placement of the lamp should be with the center of the base about in line with the shoulder, and 20 inches left or right of the book center. Wall lamps are preferred for small rooms with furniture that is close to doors and windows. Recommended shade dimensions are: top 6 to 8 inches, bottom 14 to 18 inches, depth 6 to 8 inches. Bulbs should be 100 to 150-watts. Placement should be in line with the shoulder, centered 20 inches left or right of the center of the book, with the lower edge at eye level. If the light is substantially behind the shoulder, center it 15 inches to the side with lower edge 47 to 49 inches above the floor.

Floor lamps should have a base height of 40 to 49 inches to the lower edge of the shade. Bulbs should be 150 or 200-watt soft-white. For lamps 40 to 42 inches from the floor to shade bottom, place in line with shoulder. For taller lamps, 43 to 49 inches, place the light 15 inches left or right of the book center and 26 inches back.

Table lamps used for reading in bed should be placed with the lower edge of the shade at eye level. Recommended shade dimensions are: bottom 15 to 17 inches, top 8 to 15 inches, depth 10 to 14 inches. Soft-white 150-200-watt bulbs should be used. Placement should be in line with the shoulder and 22 inches to left or right of book center. Extended arm wall lamps or fixtures centered 2 feet from the wall will span wide

A bit of ingenuity and lighting combine to create this youngster's display-play-mirror wall. The top left tackboard is illuminated by 12-volt 25R14 bulbs in painted orange juice cans. The top right shelf is lighted by two F20T12 bulbs with ½-inch eggcrate louvers. Two lower shelves using F15T8 bulbs have diffusing plastic tops. Shelf height is 2½ inches. Channels have a convenience outlet. The mirror is lighted with plug-in sockets placed every 6 inches on the vertical wire mold. Underneath the mirror are the switches and the cord, which plugs into a convenience outlet. Over the bed is a bracket containing two 40-watt fluorescents which provide 25 footcandles for reading.

headboards to bring light to the desired location. Bulbs should be 100, 150, or 200-watt. Placement is the same as for table lamps.

Fluorescent wall brackets should vary in length according to bed size as follows: single bed, one 36-inch 30-watt deluxe warm-white tube; single bed in a corner, an around-the-corner bracket using two 30-watt 36-inch deluxe warm-white tubes; double bed, one 48-inch 40-watt deluxe warm-white tube; king-size bed or twin beds, two 36-inch or two 48-inch tubes mounted end-to-end as a single unit. Locate the bracket so that the lower edge of the faceboard will be 30 inches above the mattress.

In selecting all types of lighting for children's rooms, keep in mind that fluorescents deliver three times as much light as incandescents for the same wattage, and last twenty times longer. Always select deluxe warm-white or deluxe cool-white for best color effects.

Attractive Sturdy Floors

In both new and existing rooms for children you are almost certain to encounter three or perhaps four basic types of materials used in floor construction—hardwood flooring, resilient materials, carpeting, and ceramic tile. Each has its own unique features plus a few drawbacks that may be worth considering if a change is desired.

Hardwood

As builders sought ways to cut costs, many newer homes were constructed without hardwood finish flooring. In these homes, the plywood underlayment was installed with the option of either resilient finish flooring or carpeting. In older homes, however, many a carpeted room hides an attractive hardwood surface that often can be put to use with a few hours of sanding and simple refinishing.

Most home hardwood floors are either oak or maple, both long-lasting species put down in long strips or squares. Some types include decorative pegs or parquet geometric patterns such as squares, rectangles, herringbone, and basketweave. In purchasing new hardwood flooring, you have the choice of unfinished or more expensive prefinished material which speeds installation and use of the completed surface.

In refinishing hardwood flooring it is advisable to rent an electric sanding machine and use it in combination with a small electric hand sander rather than tackle the job totally by hand. This will save time and mess in removing old finish and restoring an unmarred surface free of scratches, stains, and other marks.

Manufacturers recommend use of No. 4 open coat sandpaper for removing varnish from hardwood flooring; No. 3 closed coat sandpaper is suitable for other finishes. A second "cut" is made with No. 0 sandpaper and the final third "cut" with No. 00 or No. 000 sandpaper.

Hardwood floors of old were really never difficult to care for, but the old-style finishes were. These floors were varnished or shellacked; as the surface coat became scratched, chipped, or worn, it required a waxing. Today you can purchase hardwood flooring that has both finish and wax factory-baked deep into the wood fibers with infrared heat. Such finishes are almost impossible to wear away. Upkeep is reduced to vacuuming when you vacuum your carpet and waxing when you shampoo your carpet.

The E.L. Bruce Co., a manufacturer of hardwood flooring, recommends a few simple methods for maintenance, especially helpful if hardwood flooring is in a child's room. Here are their suggestions:

- Food spots—wipe them immediately with a damp (not wet) cloth; if the surface area then looks dull, rub on a little wax.
- White spots—usually too much wax is the problem; use fine steel wool dampened with wax or mineral spirits and then wipe dry and rub on a little wax.
- Water spots—try the white spot remedy; if it does not work, try fine sandpaper, wipe with mineral spirits, touch up with matching stain, and wax.
- Dark spots—try white or water spot treatment, or apply household bleach to the spot and let it stand for about an hour; rinse with a wet cloth, wipe dry, smooth with steel wool or fine sandpaper, touch up with matching stain, and wax.
- Ink stains—try household bleach or oxalic acid from the drug store, or lightly sand, wash with mineral spirits, retouch with stain, and then wax.
- Greasy spots—rub grease, tar, or oil with a cloth or fine steel wool dampened with mineral spirits;

Ceramic tile sheets make it possible for the homeowner to include colorful ceramic tile in children's rooms, applying the material to any flat, clean, sound surface with an adhesive. The sheets are factory grouted with silicone rubber. Of the patterns shown here, the top four are for walls, and the lower four are for floors. Photo courtesy of American Olean Tile Company

this usually lifts lipstick, crayon, and rubber marks, too.

Resilient Sheet or Tile

Resilient flooring has long been popular in children's rooms and even more so now with the introduction of the vinyl materials that require no waxing. Literally hundreds of colors and patterns are available for bedrooms, playrooms, attics, basements, and other places inhabited by children.

Sheet-vinyl flooring now comes in 6, 9, and 12-foot widths to eliminate the need for seams in most rooms. The material often has a built-in cushioned layer, and in some instances can be installed wall to wall without adhesive.

The low cost factor of sheet-vinyl flooring (and other resilient materials) makes it possible for the budget-minded to more easily decorate for a child's successive life cycles. For example, parents can select nursery colors and scenes featuring animals or toys, and later change to sports and teenage motifs at a reasonable cost.

Ceramic Tile

Ceramic tile, once confined primarily to bathroom floors and kitchen countertops, now can be found throughout the home—even in children's rooms. This material is so old that it predates western history, yet so new that usage continues to increase substantially each year.

Much of the reason for the increased popularity of ceramic tile can be attributed to its pattern and color, availability of larger size units than the standard 4¼-inch squares and the advent of colored tile grout. Decorators readily use this material for bedrooms, family rooms, and outdoor patio and play areas in addition to its use on floors, walls, and countertops in kitchens and bathrooms.

Ceramic tile is a mixture of clays that are baked at extremely high temperature to make the shape permanent. When the color is sprayed on before the mixture goes into the kiln for firing, it is called glazed tile. When the color goes all the way through the body, it is either quarry tile (which comes in natural clay colors) or ceramic mosaics (clay mixed with natural pigment). No matter what the color, the tile from the kiln is permanent, beautiful, waterproof, and simple to clean.

Many homeowners prefer to leave tile installation to the professionals, but this material is certainly not too complicated for the do-it-yourselfer to work with. A complete set of tile installation tools can be rented from your tile dealer for a few dollars, and he will provide you with detailed written instructions for accomplishing your specific task.

Cushioned vinyl floor that comes folded like a blanket and installs with a staple gun takes much of the previous work out of installing a new floor in a child's room. The do-it-yourselfer can trim the material less than perfectly but still obtain a perfect fit—the material can be stretched. This material also can be cemented to concrete surfaces. Photo courtesy of Armstrong Cork Company

You can install ceramic tile over most any structurally sound, dry, clean and level surface such as double-wood flooring, ½-inch exterior type plywood, ceramic tile, steel-troweled cement, asphalt or vinyl tile, or sheet flooring. Loose and damaged plaster, wallpaper, and paint should be removed before tiling. Grease should be removed, newly plastered walls sealed, and glossy or painted surfaces sanded.

Carpeting

Carpet experts suggest a one-two-three method of selecting carpeting or rugs for children's rooms as well as all other spaces in the home. First, decide on the color; next, choose the texture; and then choose the fiber according to the performance that is needed.

Carpet color can be one of the most versatile elements in room decorating and opens countless possibilities suggested by a quick glance at the familiar color wheel. Warm colors—yellow, orange, and red—can make a room seem smaller or make a sunless room cozier. The cool colors—green, blue, and lilac—make a room seem larger and more spacious and can cool down a very sunny exposure.

Interior designers will urge you to select your floor color first and then coordinate the rest of your draperies, walls, furniture, and accessories with it.

Carpet Fiber Characteristics The Carpet and

Rug Institute reports that wool remains a traditional leader in higher-priced and luxury lines. It resists soil and is easy to clean. It is warm, resilient, soft, and comfortable.

Nylon carpet wears exceptionally well, dyes easily and is colorfast, resists soil and is easy to clean. Acrylic looks and feels like wool, is lightweight, has fluffy pile, and cleans well. Polyester is a soft, but durable, fiber that makes excellent shag carpeting. It has low-static tendencies and is high in ease-of-care characteristics. Olefin, excellent for children's baths, kitchens, laundries, and outdoor use, has great strength and resists stain and soil. Colors are bright, clear and sharp, and static build-up is low.

Sound Control Teenagers and their love of loud music have done much to enhance the selection of carpeting not only to floors but also to walls and even to ceilings.

It is a well-accepted fact that walking on a carpeted floor produces less noise than walking on any other type of flooring. Further acoustical laboratory studies have shown that carpeting and rugs help absorb three types of noise: airborne, floor surface, and impact. The voice carries, echoes, and produces a very loud sound in an empty room—this is airborne noise. The sound of metal nails in the heels of shoes on tile floors can be distracting—this is floor surface noise. The thud of something hitting a wooden floor is a common sound—this is impact noise.

Quantity Needed One of the first questions which will have to be answered when shopping for a new carpet is the size of the area to be covered. It is a good idea to prepare a sketch with exact measurements of the area to be carpeted before visiting your local carpet retailer. This sketch can be made on plain paper, but graph paper ruled in small squares is even easier to use.

A long measuring tape should be used to obtain room dimensions. If a yardstick is used, it is a good idea to remeasure the area to avoid errors. All measurements should be in feet, and all inches less than one foot should be dropped and the total number of feet increased by one. For example, 21 feet and 10½ inches should be changed to 22 feet.

Multiplying the number of feet in one direction by the number of feet in the other will give the total number of square feet. If the total number of square feet is divided by 9, this will give the minimum number of square yards needed to cover the area. It is quite likely the amount of carpeting needed will be slightly larger than this minimum amount.

Most carpeting is made 12 feet wide, but some is produced in other widths. If the room measures 11 feet by 14 feet then the minimum square yards would be a little over 17 (11 feet × 14 feet = 154 square feet; 154 square feet divided by 9 feet = number of square

yards). However, in order to install this minimum amount, seaming of small pieces at one end would be necessary. This would probably not only be more costly due to additional cost of installation, but the many seams would look unsightly. Therefore, the amount of carpeting normally used would be 18⅔ square yards (12 feet × 14 feet divided by 9), so one piece of carpeting, without seams, could be installed. Even though it may be a little more costly for the carpeting, the end result would be well worth it. This is the reason for having a sketch as well as dimensions when buying carpeting. If the carpeting has a pattern and seams have to be made, additional carpeting will be needed to match the pattern.

In figuring the amount of carpeting you'll need for your child's room you should take into consideration bay windows, closets, doorways, and other additional areas. These areas may be small and the amount of carpeting needed to cover them may seem insignificant, but if they are not taken into consideration they may end up not covered, or the result may be poor placement of a seam.

If a room is wider than the width of the carpeting, then a seam will be required. A sketch is helpful in planning the best place to locate this seam.

A sketch is also helpful if an area rug or room-size rug is to be purchased. The size of the rug can be drawn on the sketch to show the area that it will cover. More specific information on floor coverings can be found in *Homeowner's Guide to Floors*.

Floor surfaces in rooms designed primarily for children can be a combination of materials. Here sculptured carpeting surrounds a "Race to the Magic Kingdom" nylon carpet which combines the recognition of familiar Walt Disney characters with favorite children's games. Photo courtesy of Jorges Carpet Mills, Inc.

Wall and Window Treatment

Wallcoverings

Color, texture, and pattern are the key elements of effective room settings, whether for children or adults. Water base paint or wallcoverings can be used to provide these elements on the wall and ceiling surfaces.

Wallpapers Wallpapers are classified as water-sensitive and water-resistant. Water-sensitive wallpapers include roller prints and screen or hand-printed papers. Roller prints are made by machine with colors applied simultaneously from one, two, or as many as twelve rollers. Prices of roller prints vary depending upon the weight and quality of paper used, the complexity of the design, and the number of yards manufactured.

Screen or hand prints are colored manually by using a separate screen for each color of the design. Since the hand process takes time and skill, these papers are expensive.

Water-resistant wallpapers include part-vinyl or all-vinyl versions that are available as plain acrylic, vinyl, foil, or flock. They are durable, rough, cleanable, last longer than regular wallpaper, and should be a preferred choice for children's rooms.

Wallpaper can be purchased unpasted or prepasted, with the latter type much preferred by homeowner applicators. Prepasted paper has a glue already applied to the back so the material can be simply dipped in water and hung. Often, however, a thin coat of wheat paste is needed, particularly at the edges. Unpasted papers can be applied with several types of paste. It is best to ask the wallpaper dealer for advice related to the specific area where you are to apply the material.

Wallpapers come in a variety of widths with a single roll covering approximately 30 to 36 square feet, regardless of varying widths and lengths. Rolls are usually packaged in two-roll bolts.

You can estimate your room requirements by measuring the distance in feet around the room, measuring the height of the walls to be covered, and multiplying the two figures. You can usually deduct one single roll of approximately 30 square feet for two standard door openings.

Most walls need some preparation before covering

them. Wallpapers will not adhere to dirt, soap, and grease. Clean papered walls with household soap powder or ammonia, and rinse with clean water. Remove old, loose wallpaper. If it is on tight, sand it down, glue down loose edges, size, and paper over it. Metallics, flocks, foils, and embossed patterns, however, cannot be papered over.

Grease and dirt should be washed off painted walls with a household detergent. Remove any loose or flaking paint and fill in all the cracks with crack filler, then sand to a smooth finish. Most paper manufacturers also recommend application of a coat of wall size, which assures an even surface for the wallpaper to adhere to. Let the size dry completely before continuing.

For new and unpainted walls, use a single coat of pigmented sealer and then coat with size. Glossy painted surfaces should be washed down with detergent, thoroughly sanded, and then covered with a brush coat of wall size before applying wallpaper.

Familiarize yourself with the steps to follow when applying the wallpaper. Most retail dealers will supply you with folders illustrating the steps involved for their particular brands. A few suggestions worthy of mention, however, are listed below.

- Always cover the ceiling before the walls. It is easier to work with shorter strips (width-wise of the room), but consider the whole room when you decide in which direction you will work.
- Never wrap a whole strip around inside corners without cutting and realigning. It may look fine at first, but in a few weeks, wrinkles and creases may appear.
- When using no-match, plain textured wallpapers, try reversing every other strip top to bottom for more uniform color.
- Never use a seam roller on flocked wallpapers. Gently tap the seams with the edge of the smoothing brush.
- Check the run numbers on your rolls before you start, to make sure they are the same, as color may vary slightly from run to run.
- Ceilings, like walls, are not always "true." So plan to end the ceiling wallpaper on the less critical side of the room, like above the entrance.
- When using the same pattern on the ceiling and

Big stenciled letters in bright, bold colors are the kind of wall decoration that will remain attractive as the child grows. Photo courtesy of 1001 Decorating Ideas Magazine

walls, it can only be matched one way—so choose the direction most noticeable.

Nearly everything you need for applying wallpaper can generally be found in the house; stepladder, yardstick, scissors, pencil, string, chalk, knife, a bucket of clean water, and a sponge. You will also need a smoothing brush and a seam and paste roller (or a waterbox if hanging prepasted wallpaper).

Paneling The availability of moderately priced do-it-yourself paneling has made any decorator's job a great deal easier. In many instances, the addition of one wall of paneling can change the entire appearance of the room.

Paneling over an existing wall is a relatively simple operation with modern materials and accessories. Standard-sized 4 × 8-foot panels are designed to speed installation and minimize necessary cutting and fitting.

Built-ins can be finished with wallcoverings just as the walls themselves. These coordinated patterns include a complete alphabet running continuously on blocks of different sized gingham checks, each 4½ inches square. Photo courtesy of James Seeman Studios, Inc.

Once you have taken delivery, stand the panels separately around the room at least forty-eight hours prior to installation to acclimate them to room conditions. (Some manufacturers recommend the panels be left flat, separated by blocks to allow air movement, so check this point when making your purchase.)

Specific installation methods vary with the type of paneling selected and the place of intended use. For example:

- Paneling any existing smooth, flat wall is accomplished using continuous ribbons of adhesive applied at specified intervals over lightly sanded enameled walls, sealed gypsum wallboard, or previously wallpapered walls.
- Paneling masonry, cement, or other unevenly surfaced walls requires application of 1×2, 2×3, or 2×4-inch furring or framing laid flat against the wall, horizontally on 16-inch centers and vertically on 48-inch centers (masonry must be waterproofed before applying the furring, and shims may be required to insure an even surface).

Each panel should be checked for plumb as it is applied to the wall surface. Most manufacturers will recommend you begin the installation in a corner. Use of a scribing compass will enable you to mark corner panels (as well as around windows and doors) for easy cutting with a coping saw. In making panel cuts with a power hand-held circular saw, always saw from the back side of the panel using a fine-tooth blade.

Matching color annular-threaded nails can be purchased for applying paneling directly to studs or for top and bottom-panel use in combination with adhesives. When adhesives are not used, nail panels every 4 inches along all edges and every 8 inches into intermediate furring.

Solid lumber paneling also can be obtained in various woods, patterns, and sizes with widths ranging from 6 to 12 inches. This material can be used vertically to make a room seem higher or installed horizontally to make a short room appear longer. Diagonal treatments, random widths, and herringbone styles are additional ways of creating unusual effects.

Wood-grain high-pressure decorative plastic laminates are available in vertical grades (as well as the more familiar countertop surfacing grades) for walls. Simulated brick and stucco-finish panels are also available. Each of these may be applied with adhesives.

Supergraphics Supergraphics or free designs are growing in popularity for home use as well as the many commercial establishments that use them for modern wall decor. These designs can move from wall to wall, floor to ceiling to direct your eye around the room, create headboards, conceal architectural deficiencies, and create truly individual centers of interest within a given area.

Both paint and wallcoverings are used by homeowners and interior designers to provide unusual color, texture, and pattern. Paint designs can be as expansive as the imagination, ranging from a simple horizontal line ending in an arrow to highly intricate geometrics.

The advent of the poster business in the 1960s brought with it innovations in printing techniques and new approaches in graphic art concepts, which in turn opened up the possibilities for the first supergraphic wallcoverings. Since that time various firms have entered the marketplace with dozens of design statements that have dramatic artistic impact and yet endure as a background for living environments.

Along with the evolution of designs, there has been an accompanying development in lithographic printing. The variety of subjects, the quality of work, and their reproduction is the result of the combined resources of artist and this advanced lithographic technology.

It is desirable to use washable paint or wallcoverings for supergraphic installations, especially in children's rooms where fingermarks are sure to occur. Wall graphics are sold as complete sets for installation over smooth surfaces coated with a white sealer. Panels are hung according to a diagram provided with each scene, and repeating graphics can be started at any place in the design.

Photomurals Photomurals have long been popular on office walls, but have now moved into many homes as well. Inspiring vistas can now be added from floor to ceiling in any room.

Some photomurals measure up to 12 feet 8 inches $\times$ 9 feet and may be trimmed for smaller walls. Installation requires just a pair of scissors, a brush or two, and the cellulose paste supplied with each lithographed view. Each mural comes precut in easy-to-hang sections, is easier to handle than wallpaper, and has a varnished surface that can be wiped clean with a wet sponge.

Mural designs available include: ocean vistas, sunsets, mountains, forests, animals, and other scenics.

If you desire a more personal approach to wall decor, Eastman Kodak, 3M Company, and Berkey Photos are among the firms that take your color transparencies (or stock views) and turn them into custom murals mounted on stiff backing for sectional installation in any room. Special lacquers are used to give a custom finish that can be washed. Still other firms and processes make possible the reproduction of full-color transparencies directly onto almost any flexible material, including fabrics, paper, and carpeting, but these are expensive alternatives.

Posters Beyond a doubt, the most popular items for

This astronomic scene is the key focal point of this young adult's bedroom furnished with a modern platform bed and molded plastic seating units. The nighttime colors are offset by a bright yellow panel at right and the panel doors, one painted deep blue and the other orange. Photo courtesy of Environmental Graphics

decorating teenagers' rooms are wall posters. Whereas children of the '40s and '50s were satisfied with 8×10-inch pinup photos of their favorite athletes or movie stars, today they prefer 30×40-inch posters. Today, there are posters for almost any age group. Popular teenage posters include musicians, movie and television personalities, and athletes. For the younger set popular subjects include cartoon characters from Walt Disney, Sesame Street and Warner Brothers, animals, doll characters, and Star Wars.

Pro Arts posters, ranging in size from 8½ by 11 inches to those covering almost 24 square feet, are sold in most every gift shop and discount store in the country.

Full-color "Signature" action posters of well-known athletes in basketball, tennis, soccer, football, base-ball, and golf are sold by *Sports Illustrated* magazine. The publication also offers a selection of skiing, sailing, and surfing posters.

Teenagers by no means are limited to heroes for their poster subject matter; a poster made from their own photo or negative can be purchased at most camera shops for $10 to $20.

Window Decor

Selection of the proper draperies, curtains, or other window accessories for a child's room begins with selection of the right hardware for your chosen window treatment.

Window decorating hardware ranges from bold and

Posters and record album covers are popular wall decorations with the younger set and can be quickly changed as one tires of viewing any scene. This family bath design by Kohler illustrates desirable countertop area, over-the-tub lighting, easy-to-clean floor, and shampoo-style lavatory bowl and fittings.

beautiful decorative rods to the more familiar conventional rods that blend into the background. In making your selection, consider the design of your window, its location, and exactly what you want it to contribute to the room.

Most bedroom windows in older homes are double-hung units, while homes built in recent years tend to have sliding windows. Other rooms may have a dormer, bay, or casement arrangement.

Interior designers stress a number of questions you should answer before you select any particular type of window covering. Included are: Should the window be dramatic or unobtrusive? Will it hide a view or frame a desirable outdoor scene? Will it be opened during the day and closed at night? Need it appear larger or smaller in the total room scheme? Will extra daylight be required for any particular purposes, such as playtime?

While windows are somewhat fixed although not impossible to replace, your decorating treatment can change their shape. Low, squat windows can be made taller by using a valance above the window and side draperies. Tier curtains can be used to make windows appear shorter or hide trouble spots.

In rooms with northern exposure, it is recommended you use warm colors such as red, orange, yellow, and their various color shades such as pink, peach, and

lemon. Cool colors, like blue, green, and violet are restful, and good choices for rooms with a southern exposure. In general, use light colors on the large areas and use bright colors as accents.

Window Rods Here's a rundown on the traditional rods available and some of their specific features.

- Conventional curtain rods—These are threaded through the heading of a sheer curtain that seldom moves and can project out from the window or fit closely. Close-fitting sash rods can be suspended with hooks or can have rubber ends, or can be spring loaded to eliminate the need for screws and nails.
- Cafe rods—These rods support curtains or draperies with movable rings. The curtains can be opened or closed by hand or baton. They can be used alone, in two or three tier combination, or with conventional draw draperies.
- Conventional traverse rods—Adjustable up to 220 inches, they are concealed from view by the heading of the draperies once closed. The draw rods can be used separately or in pairs for combining draperies with shirred curtains.

Draperies Today the selection of drapery material is greater than ever. You can choose from numerous textures, patterns, colors, and built-in features. It is possible to select satin, openweave, velvet, cotton, linen or almost any other fabric or texture you can think of in draperies that are unlined, self-lined, lined with cotton, or backed with insulating foam. Major department stores and smaller specialty shops offer draperies in several styles including ready-made, precision, made-to-measure, and fully custom-made. Also consider making your own.

Ready-made draperies generally are pleated to 75 percent of fullness (1½ times) and come in various dimensions. Precision-made draperies are ordered in standard widths hemmed to within an inch of the length you specify. Made-to-measure draperies differ from fully custom-made in that you take the measurements to the store for the former, and a drapery expert does the measuring for the latter.

Curtains Curtains are usually made of sheer or semisheer fabrics in shorter lengths than draperies. Only tailored curtain panels and Priscilla curtains are more than 45 inches long. Priscilla curtains are very much at home with traditional decor. They are sheer or semiopaque, and come in widths up to 300 inches per pair. To crisscross them, multiply the area to be covered by four to determine correct size. (See accompanying chart for stacking-area of draperies.) Widths are limited, and the curtains usually come in just one width with a flat unpleated top.

Colorful novelty curtains are very popular for children's rooms, and almost all are made of easy-care

Stacking Area Chart. *The stacking area is the space taken up by the draperies when fully open. For a complete view of your window, plan to have the stacking area against the wall on either side of the window glass. Use this chart to determine stacking area for standard glass sizes.*

To determine stacking area for odd-sized windows, measure glass width, divide by three, and add 12 inches. This measurement is your stacking area. Add the stacking area to the glass measurement to get your rod measurement. Make sure this measurement is within the measurement printed on the box. Divide your stacking area by two. Place brackets this distance on either side of glass.

If your draperies are one-way, extend the rod the full stacking area on one side only. For bulky fabric, add 4 to 10 inches to the stacking area measurement.

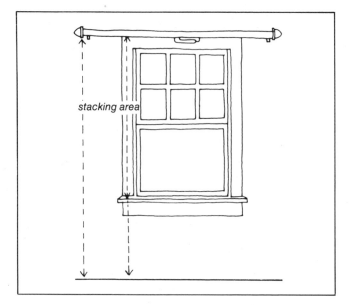

Tips for easier drapery hardware installation:

1. *Avoid the miter joint if mounting hardware on the casing. Place screws above or below the joint.*

2. *If mounting on a hollow wall, use special fastening devices such as Molly screw anchors, plastic screw anchors, or toggle bolts. Use 1¼-inch wood screws if you can locate wood studs.*

3. *If using one support, place at center of rod. If using two or more supports, space somewhat equally across the rod but nearer the brackets to support weight of stacked draperies. In some instances, supports are specifically used for inside or outside rod. Check the instructions.*

4. *The length of adjustable or cut-to-measure conventional traverse or curtain rods is the space between brackets, including brackets.*

5. *The length of adjustable decorative cafe and decorative traverse rods does not include the finial measurement. If near a corner wall, be sure the finial will fit. Rings are not included with decorative cafe rods.*

6. *Cord tension pulleys are recommended for use with longer length traverse rods to keep cords taut and off the floor and to eliminate tangled cords.*

7. *Most conventional traverse rods are adaptable to ceiling installation. Instruction sheets for mounting these rods on the ceiling are packaged with them.*

DETERMINING THE STACKING AREA OF DRAPERIES

Glass width	Stacking area	Rod measurement	Bracket distance on either side of glass
36″	24″	60″	12″
48″	28″	76″	14″
60″	32″	92″	16″
72″	36″	108″	18″
84″	40″	124″	20″
96″	44″	140″	22″
108″	48″	156″	24″
120″	52″	172″	26″
132″	56″	188″	28″
144″	60″	204″	30″
156″	64″	220″	32″
168″	68″	236″	34″
180″	72″	252″	36″
192″	76″	268″	38″
204″	80″	284″	40″
216″	84″	300″	42″

Tools needed. *Your tools will be a yardstick or steel tape measure (cloth tape stretches), a sharp pair of shears, needles and pins, a thimble, a strong thread in the proper color, and iron and pressing board, and, if you have one, a sewing machine.*

A large working space, such as a broad table or a clean floor, is also essential.

For the best results use good materials, measure accurately, and align patterns carefully.

Cutting first width. *Before you do anything, cut selvages away or pink and clip them so the seams will not pucker and the draperies will hang straight.*

For ease in working with material and to guard against costly mistakes, lay your fabric on a large flat surface when cutting. To insure correct cuts and proper hanging, begin with a true crosswise grain. Do not tear across fabric. In sheer fabrics, pull a thread to see the grain, then cut along its line. In patterned fabric cut evenly across the pattern. Mark and cut the fabric at the same length measurement that you determined when you planned the amount of fabric you would need (length plus hem and top and pattern repeat).

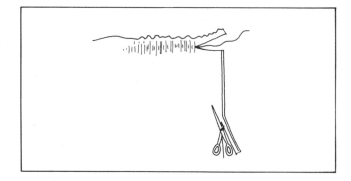

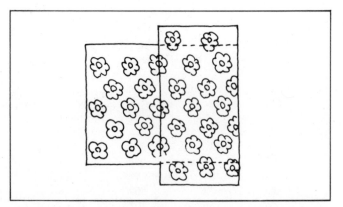

Cutting subsequent widths. *Once you have cut the first width, lay it on top of the fabric remaining to be cut so the pattern matches. Pin all around, then cut the second width. Repeat until you have cut all the widths. Remember, not only must each panel and each side of a pair of curtains match, but every window in the room should match according to pattern.*

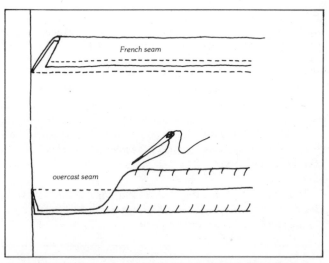

French seam

overcast seam

Joining widths into panels. *To avoid a raw edge when joining widths into panels, use a narrow French seam or overcast both edges of the seam. Drawings courtesy Kenney Manufacturing Company*

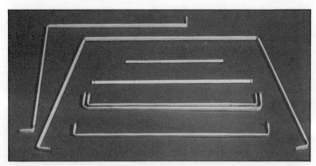

Curtain rods (in top to bottom order) can be purchased to accomplish a specific decorating job including: corner window, bay window, sash rod, spring-pressure curtain rod, double curtain rod, and single curtain rod. Photo courtesy of Kirsch Company

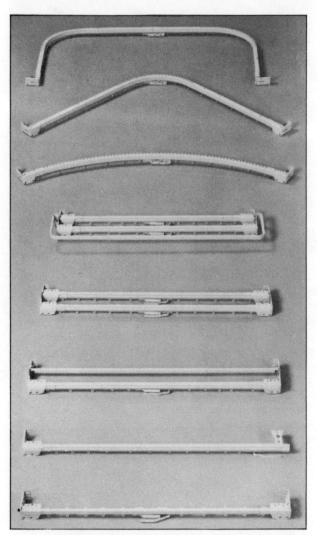

Conventional traverse rods come in a variety of styles, from top to bottom, including: cut-to-measure for rectangular bay, cut-to-measure for corner window, cut-to-measure for bow window, double traverse with valance rod, double traverse, traverse and curtain rod set, one-way-draw traverse and two-way-draw traverse. Photo courtesy of Kirsch Company

fibers. A lot of these curtains have many variations available for creating your own effects.

Panels are almost always sheer polyester. White and ecru are traditional favorites, but other colors are now available. Some panels have intricate designs and embroidery.

Woven-Wood Shades Another type of window treatment that is rapidly growing in popularity is the woven-wood shade which comes in a myriad of colors. These units roll like fabric or double fold from either top or bottom. Some can even be used as draw draperies or used as cafe curtains or folding doors.

Outside mounting of woven-wood shades usually allows a three-inch larger surrounding dimension than the window itself for prevention of a light gap. Inside or recessed mounting is done within the window frame, usually with a valance hiding the mounting elements.

Play Areas — Indoors and Out

Playrooms

A playroom unless properly planned can create additional work for parents in addition to failing in its intended purpose. All playrooms are subjected to hard use, continual abuse, spills, stains, strewn toys, and high-spirited noise.

If the playroom cannot take wear and tear, it will age rapidly. With good planning, however, a playroom can serve a succession of children for a number of years. At the end of this period, there will still be the basic walls, floor, ceiling, and built-ins that can be redecorated for new functions.

Planning Considerations To make a playroom as usable as possible, the room should have the following features:

- Durability—Since walls and floors take a great deal of abuse, they should be covered with strong materials. Prefinished hardboard panels which are virtually childproof are a good choice for walls because they will not dent, mar, or scuff. Stains and soils (including crayon, chalk, and fingermarks) wash off easily. A wide variety of finishes are available including: warm wood grains, cheery colors, and attractive patterns. For floors, choose a resilient covering, preferably one with a no-wax finish that is easy to clean with soap and water, or consider the use of washable carpet squares that can be easily replaced if damaged.

- Storage—Playrooms need plenty of storage area. Built-in units with tabletop space and undercounter cabinets work well. Durable plastic laminates in wood tones, bright colors or patterns can add to the decorative theme and at the same time require minimum upkeep. Another practical idea is a storage wall of perforated hardboard paneling. These panels have holes which accept hooks on which a variety of items can be hung and brackets on which to mount shelves. Hooks and shelves set low on the wall are easy for small children to reach, so playroom items are more likely to be put away. Also, youngsters like to have their favorite toys on display and readily accessible.

- Sound-conditioning—This is more easily and economically achieved than most people realize. A number of acoustical ceiling materials are available for sound-control. Use of heavy drapery and carpeting or cushioned flooring helps deaden noise transmission to the rest of the house. What you put on the walls also makes a difference. Even hardboard paneling makes a good sound insulator.

It is most important that the furniture used in the playroom is scaled to the size of the youngster. Small table-and-chair sets will prompt more enjoyable playtime than the standard higher table and chairs used by adults.

Playroom Suggestions Children especially like modular boxes which can be arranged and rearranged at will. These units are easily constructed from plywood, painted bright colors, and serve many functions. Such boxes can be seats, tables, blocks, storage cubicles, and other imaginary items.

Sprawling train and car racetrack setups can be made more usable and enjoyable by securing the track

Tote-boxes long have been used by adults for numerous tasks about the home. This one is designed specifically for the child, made of plywood, and painted a bright red. It has two convenient compartments, one with a door and the other with a window. Photo courtesy of American Plywood Association

A fun carpet quickly established the setting for this family playroom where countless games can be enjoyed while relaxing on the floor. Among the games are chess, checkers, hopscotch, Parcheesi, tic-tac-toe, and spinout. The colorful carpeting resists wear and soil and comes complete with component game kits. Photo courtesy of Jorges Carpet Mills, Inc.

Playhouses don't have to be elaborate, expensive structures. A child's imagination can make a castle out of a few simple materials, such as hay bales and old discarded pallets.

to a sheet of plywood hinged at the base of a wall. When not in use, the panel can be raised via pulleys until it is parallel with the wall and out of the traffic pattern.

Here are some other successful playroom ideas:

- Use chalkboard-finish hardboard for the tabletop and mount it on legs at a height where children can sit on it and draw.
- Include sections of tackboard on the walls of the room so youngsters can create their own decor with finished crayon drawings, paste-ups, and other artwork.
- Use open-front bookcases for doll houses, each shelf being a different room or floor in the home.
- Build storage chests to foam-mattress size to provide a naptime corner.
- Equip undercounter storage sections with casters so the child can move the entire contents to another place in the room.
- If a television set is to be included in the room, place it on a swivel table so it can be directed at various play areas within the room.

Playhouses

Do not build a playhouse scaled for three-year-olds if your children are nine and ten. Three-foot ceilings are fine for tiny tots but create cramped quarters for a ten-year-old.

The most successful playhouses are often designed by the children who use them. An adult hand is sometimes required to transport a 100-pound bag of sand to the backyard, dig a 4-foot-deep posthole for a swing, or nail the roof rafters to the wall frame of the tree house. Even when the job demands your skill and strength, be sure to keep the children involved. Why not sit down and design that special playhouse with them?

First, sketch a map of your backyard or patio. Make some simple cutouts of the structures you and the children have in mind (exercise equipment and sandboxes as well as playhouses). Once you've got the right layout, which has a tendency to change as time passes, start building some miniature mockups. The models you and the kids build do not have to be fancy. Use cardboard, paper clips, rubber cement, construction paper, tongue depressors, pipe cleaners, toothpicks joined by modeling clay—whatever materials are available and fun to work with. If you and your children agree on a big project, draw up blueprints in the fall, build models in the winter, and then do the actual construction in the spring and summer.

Participating in this type of family project stimulates a child's creativity and imagination and, more

Playhouses can provide a variety of activities and stimulate a child's imagination in any climate at any time of year. Photo courtesy of Child Life Play Specialties

This structure can be many things to a child: a fortress, mountain, castle tower, cave, tunnel and dungeon. The structure can double as a storage facility for trikes, wagons and other toys. Photo courtesy of California Redwood Association

important, being involved builds self-confidence in kids. When you work with your children, you are telling them, "You're important. I want to hear your ideas, and I want you to hear my ideas. Together we're a great team."

Looking for Materials Use readily available materials to construct your playhouse. Local businesses and tradespeople may even be trying to get rid of the materials you are searching for. A few possibilities include the following:

- Carpet stores. Need something warm to put down on the floor of your tipi or Mongolian yurt? A local carpet outlet may have just the right number of discontinued rug samples. You may even be able to obtain larger scrap pieces, thereby saving yourself the trouble of stitching smaller pieces together. Foam underpadding remnants are also often available.

- Construction sites. These are better known as the poor man's lumberyards. Nails, studs, siding, Sheetrock, 4 × 4s—you name it, and you will probably find it wherever new homes, apartments, or businesses are being built. The materials may not be in perfect condition, but you and your family can put them back into good shape with little effort.

- Gas stations. Inner tubes, tire casings, bottle caps, and other discards can be picked up free at garages. If you live in the country and know a farmer, you can make a fabulous sandbox from an old, discarded tractor tire or make a sturdy swing from a truck tire.

- Telephone companies. Occasionally you can pick up an old telephone set, the perfect addition to any playhouse. Scrap telephone wire is always plentiful and available. Have your name put on the wooden-cable-spool waiting list. These spools make good tables and are fantastic structures for rolling and climbing. If you are lucky enough to get a large one, you can even turn it into a round house.

- Lumber companies. Mounds of wood scraps are given away for the asking. Bizarre-looking curls of wood can dress up the plainest playhouses.

- Moving companies. Overseas moving companies occasionally discard large packing crates. These units are generally well built and make excellent playhouse frames. Keep your eyes peeled for fiberboard drums that movers use to store items.
- Home. If it has been a while since you last cleaned out the garage and closets, your home probably contains an array of useful items for creative building—old hats, shoes, paper-towel rolls, buttons, spools, juice cans, empty plastic detergent bottles, magazines, newspapers, egg cartons, and aluminum pie plates. Assorted play props encourage kids to explore and experiment: inclines for rolling and pushing; boards and teeters for balancing; pulleys, pumps, and springs for inventing perpetual motion machines. Work with a variety of materials and create surfaces that are warm to the touch, textured, rough, cold, soft, or hard. Textures are an important growing experience for a younger child.

Deciding on the Structure How permanent do you want the playhouse to be? Will the structure go up on a Saturday and come down on the following Sunday? Will it be a play space to last for years? If your children are still preschoolers and you are thinking of moving within a year, do not build an elaborate miniature house that will become a permanent part of the landscape. Something easy to put up, take down, and transport to the new home, like a tipi, would be more sensible.

- Consider the land. Regardless of how simple or complex the play structure, try to blend it in with the existing natural features of your yard. Take advantage of the slopes, rock outcroppings, and vegetation. Stepping logs or stones on a slope can create varied climbing terrain and hours of motor skill development for your youngsters. Use the existing landforms to help you direct the flow of play and add visual gaiety as well as a feeling of intimacy to play areas.
- Climate. How will your structures stand up under changing climate conditions? What steps can you take to assure the playhouse's durability? Will the installation of drainage ditches or the addition of waterproof coverings help? Think in terms, also, of the micro-climate of your particular yard. In order to provide for play that is fun and healthful, you will have to allow for reasonable amounts of sun, shade, and protection from the wind.
- Defining territory. Decide what part of your yard belongs to you and what part belongs to the children. A sense of territoriality is important to children. The playhouse should be a place they can go to get away from the pressures of homework and parental demands.

If possible, try to position the play units of older children (eight years and up) out of sight of the main house. At this age, they are beginning to vigorously assert their own personalities, and they need opportunities to be physically apart from their parents. The spatial needs of the under-five child, however, are much more limited. Their play area should be within sight and shouting distance of the house and in an area protected from motor traffic. If your children are physically or emotionally handicapped, you may want to locate their play space closer to the main house regardless of age. Skillful placement and design of playhouses and exercise apparatus can make children unaware of their parents' proximity, fostering feelings of independence. Children with mental retardation and brain injuries, as well as those with neuromuscular and orthopedic handicaps, generally need more closely contained areas to allow for easier monitoring.

- Keep imagination in mind. Leave part of the design open so that your children can add onto it and grow with the structure. You can build the basic frame (sink the corner posts of an A-frame into the ground) and let the kids put up the siding, paint, and decorate. Allow their creative imaginations free rein.

Young children have different needs and skill levels than older children. This structure is designed specifically for small children to help develop basic skills such as climbing stairs, sliding and using a pulley. Drawing courtesy of Canadian Children's Environment Advisory Service

Furniture

Let the youngsters build their own furniture. They can do it without being master craftsmen. Every day millions of people discard items that appear useless; but when viewed through knowing eyes, these materials are ideal building supplies. Some attractive and long-lasting playhouse furniture has been pieced together with discarded wooden boxes.

Circus toys are playroom favorites and provide movable storage to encourage the youngster to pick up at the end of playtime. Photo courtesy of American Plywood Association

INSTRUCTIONS FOR CIRCUS WAGON:

1. *Trace cutting and painting patterns onto plywood. Some patterns are complete. Others, like the pieces R on the Circus Wagon, must be flopped over to trace the second half of the pattern. The cutting pattern for the Circus Wagon is represented by a solid line. (The thinner lines identify the areas to be painted.) The cutting patterns and paint diagrams can be traced on the plywood. Then turn the paper pattern over and repeat the process to obtain the full pattern for each piece.*
2. *Cut out the plywood pieces and assemble the box, gluing and nailing as required. Ornamentation will be added later.*
3. *Drill a 1½-inch hole in each H piece as shown. Glue-nail the four H pieces to the bottom of the wagon. Glue and screw the wheels and hubcaps together. Glue six evenly spaced spokes to each wheel. Insert the 1½-inch axle dowels through the holes and attach wheel apparatus (including spacers) as shown.*
4. *Drill a 1¼-inch hole in each K piece for the dowel. Glue and screw the K pieces to the front of the cart. Insert the dowel. Glue and screw the top and bottom handle I pieces to the dowel.*
5. *Glue ornamentation in appropriate places as shown.*
6. *Fill any gaps in exposed plywood edges with wood dough. Sand smooth when dry.*
7. *Finish with latex paint.*

You need not rummage around in the garbage to find discards. Ask a store owner if there are any packing materials he intends to throw away. Offer to cart them away yourself, saving him time and labor—a great trade for everyone involved. Have you noticed any old peach or pear crates lying by the fruit bins of your local supermarket? With a few nails or screws and a bit of fresh paint, the children can put together storage shelves for their tree house or playhouse.

You can create just about anything you or your children can imagine from these leftover wooden crates, cardboard boxes, and fiberboard drums. They make excellent chairs, tables, beds, desks, bookshelves, easels, stools, storage chests, couches, or partitions.

Tipis (commonly spelled tepees)

The word tipi comes from the Sioux language. "Ti" means to dwell or live and "pi" means used for. According to many authorities, the tipi of the American Plains Indian is the most practical, movable dwelling ever invented. It can be pitched in fifteen minutes by an experienced individual, it is extremely roomy and well ventilated being cool in summer and warm and dry in winter, it is well lighted, and it can withstand severe winds and heavy downpours.

Indian children often built their own tipis under their mother's direction. Exact replicas of their parent's nomadic dwellings, these miniature tipis served as playhouses.

Helping your youngsters build an authentic tipi playhouse is a fascinating and exciting history lesson

---

MATERIALS

Quantity	Description
1 panel	½ inch × 4 foot × 8-foot plywood*
12	2 inch × ⅜-inch carriage bolts
11 feet	½-inch dowel cut in nine 13½-inch lengths (remaining dowel can be cut in two 3-inch pieces for chair cushion)
4	3-inch butt hinges
As required	6d finishing nails
As required	Wood dough, fine sandpaper, white or urea-resin glue, top-quality latex paint

*Recommended plywood: A-B Interior, A-C Exterior, or Medium Density Overlaid (MDO) APA® grade-trademarked plywood

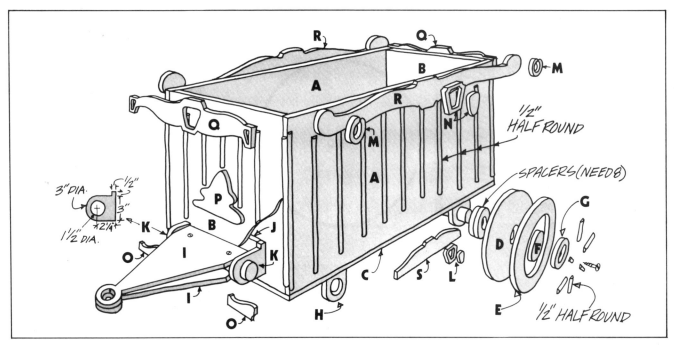

1. Exploded view

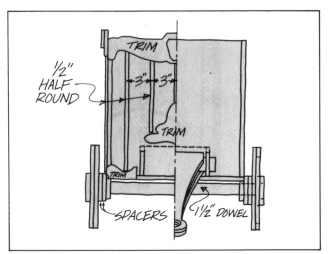

2. Front view

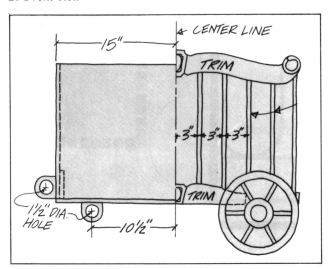

3. Side view

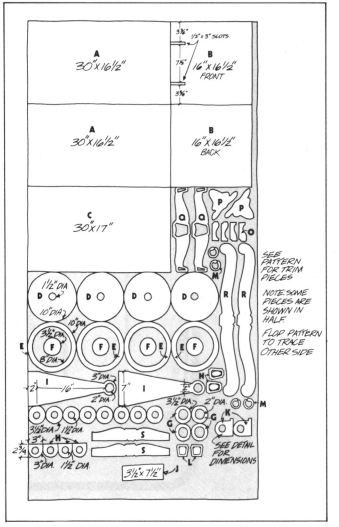

4. Panel layout

INSTRUCTIONS FOR SEAL CHAIR AND CAGE DESK:

1. *Trace the cutting and painting patterns onto the plywood. The cutting pattern for the Seal Chair and Cage Desk is represented by the gray area.*

2. *Carefully cut out the plywood pieces.*

3. *Desk assembly: First cut four 1-inch × 3½-inch blocks from the scrap plywood. Glue-nail blocks and optional lip detail to desk top as indicated. Notch the ½-inch dowels on both ends as shown, and glue-nail in place on desk front and sides. Attach butt hinges to desk front and sides. Align desk top and sides. Then drill carriage bolt holes through desk sides into desk top blocks as shown. After the four main carriage bolt holes are drilled, drill two additional holes below each top hole on desk sides. Bolt desk sides and top together, using the appropriate side hole to adjust the desk to your child's height.*

4. *Chair assembly: First cut oblong holes in chair back and seat pieces as shown. Then cut four 1 inch × 3½-inch seat supports and four 1 inch × 3½-inch back supports from scrap plywood. Glue-nail seat and back supports in positions indicated. Align seal chair sides with chair back. Then drill carriage bolt holes through seal sides into back support blocks. Insert carriage bolts. Align seat with seal sides, and drill through seal sides into seat supports. Assemble chair by fastening remaining carriage bolts in place.*

5. *Fill any plywood edge gaps with wood dough. Sand smooth when dry.*

6. *Finish with top-quality latex paint. Suggested colors are identified on exploded views. When paint is dry, install seat cushion if desired.*

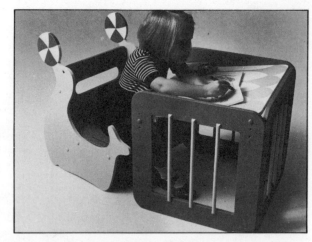

Easy-to-make furniture such as this all-plywood desk-seat arrangement prompts playtime activity far more than having the youngster sit at the kitchen table. Photo courtesy of American Plywood Association

MATERIALS

Quantity	Description
1 panel	½ inch × 4 foot × 8-foot plywood*
37 feet	½-inch half-rounds cut to various lengths for ornamentation
4½ feet	½-inch half-rounds for spokes (cut in 2¼-inch lengths)
43 inches	1½-inch dowel for axles (cut in two 21½-inch pieces)
10 inches	1¼-inch dowel for attaching handle to wagon
As required	#6 wood screws
As required	6d finishing nails
As required	White or urea-resin glue, wood dough, fine sandpaper, top-quality latex paint

*Recommended plywood: A-B Interior, A-C Exterior, or Medium Density Overlaid (MDO) APA® grade-trademarked plywood.

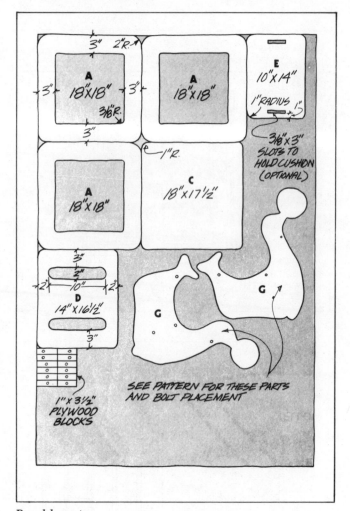

Panel layout

on our native American culture. You can make the pattern for a tipi cover by sewing together 36-inch-wide strips of canvas. Up until the late 1870s, the Plains Indians fashioned their nomadic cones from buffalo hide. When the great herds of buffalo began to wane, the Indians turned to canvas. Today there are many types of canvas to choose from. Some of them, such as marine and treated army duck, are rainproof and mildew resistant, but quite expensive. You might consider buying a less expensive 10 or 12-ounce canvas and treating it yourself with a quality water repellent. It is recommended that you treat both sides of the canvas (you will need 2 to 4 gallons). If yours is not a flame-retardant fabric, it should be treated with Chex-flame.

Real tipis have two layers, the outside cover and an inside dew liner. The liner is approximately 4 to 5 feet high and is hung completely around the inside of the tipi. It seals to the ground. This dew cloth provides excellent insulation and ventilation. It keeps the tipi dry and comfortable inside. You can make the liner out of the same canvas used for the cover.

INSTRUCTIONS FOR BUILDING A TIPI:

1. You will need thirteen poles, nine in the frame, two for the smoke flaps, one to hoist the canvas into place, and one to hold fast the smoke flap cords. Frame and hoisting poles should each be 11 feet long, smoke flap poles 9 feet, and the smoke flap cord pole 4 feet. Cedar, lodgepole, or Douglas fir are best. The poles must be straight, no thicker than 3 inches at the butt and tapering to 1 inch at the top. Peel the bark and dry each pole before using. If you do not have access to unmilled wood, 2×4s can be cut diagonally from end to end and substituted as poles.

2. Lay the three stoutest poles on the tipi cover. The butts of the two rear poles both go directly to the rear, and the butt of the front pole goes to the side (crosswise from the door). All three poles cross at the tie point.

3. Secure the tripod of poles at the tie point with one end of a 35-foot length of rope. Begin with a clove hitch, then finish off the binding with three wrappings and one final clove hitch.

4. Lift up the tripod and walk under the poles, pushing up the bound tops. Once the poles are upright, spread the two back poles so that the three are locked in position.

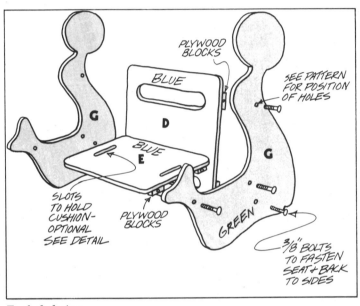

Exploded view

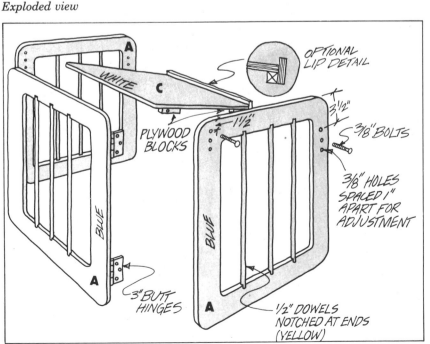

Exploded view

Seat details

5. Now put the remaining poles, with the exception of the lifting pole and the two smaller flap poles, in the frame. Position these seven poles so that they are evenly spaced around the tripod.

6. Tightly wrap the 35-foot length of rope four times around the poles. Anchor the free end of the rope at or near the center point of the tipi's floor.

7. Next tie two ropes at the tie point of the canvas cover to the top end of the lifting pole. Hoist the entire bundle, pole and folded canvas, by setting the butt of the pole at the tipi's back (directly opposite the door) and walking it up.

8. Unroll the cover around the poles so that the two canvas sides meet at the front.

9. Lace down the front of the tipi starting at the top near the smoke flaps.

10. Reposition the poles so that the cover fits snugly, then peg the canvas to the ground.

11. Finally, fasten the smoke flap tie-cords to the two remaining poles.

At first glance, the finished tipi playhouse may surprise you. The dwelling is not a perfectly symmetrical cone; in fact, a cross section of the tipi reveals that it is egg shaped! Real tipis are tilted cones with longer front sides than back sides — and for sound reasons. When the back of the tipi is placed against prevailing winds, the structure can withstand the strongest gale. The tilted cone-shape also gives you more headroom at the back for standing and playing space.

Indians decorated both the outside and the inside of their tipis. You can do the same, preferably before the canvas is hoisted into place. The children can sew or paint their designs. Even crayon drawings can be made and then melted into the fabric with the aid of brown wrapping paper and a hot clothes iron.

Indians use colors, shapes, and designs symbolically; for example, among some tribes, circles represent

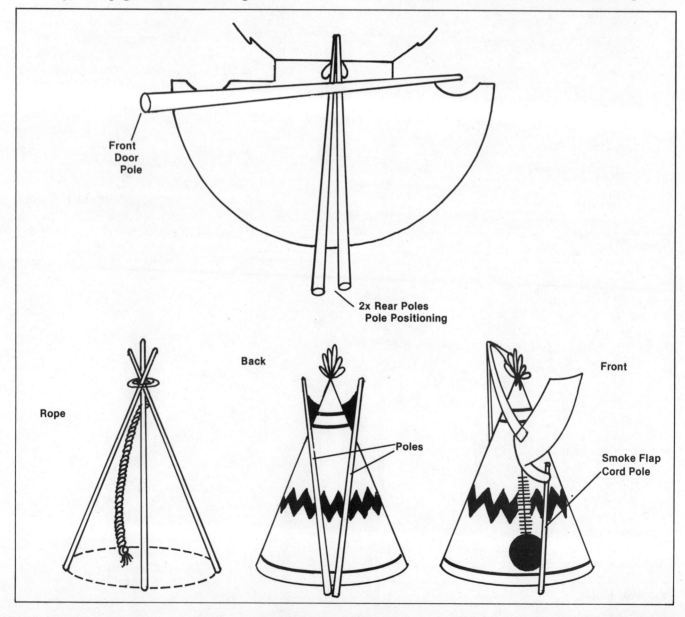

Front Door Pole

2x Rear Poles Pole Positioning

Rope

Back

Poles

Front

Smoke Flap Cord Pole

Play areas can be created along property lines in many areas where high fences are permitted by the city building department. Here the play platform and walkway were constructed of 2×4-inch Douglas fir while wood chips were used as the ground cover to keep down weeds, dust, and eliminate tracking mud into the house. The low fence in the foreground is a pleasant background for landscaping as well as a partial screen between the play area and lawn area of the yard. Photo courtesy of Western Wood Products Association

the sun. A red circle symbolizes the morning sun, a yellow circle the setting sun; a triangle represents a tipi; a zig-zagging line (lightning) signals a storm; bear paws communicate wisdom, magic, and medicine.

Play Yards

Ideas for home play yards for children are almost as numerous as the parents who plan them, and, also as diverse. Many parents are of the opinion that children should be almost totally unstructured in their outdoor play. On the other side is the argument that planned play spaces help to direct the child in learning and keep him from being bored.

Both approaches have good points and may be incorporated into any area of the yard set aside for children's use. The age of the children, of course, further dictates what can be done, as does the geographic location and the yard size.

If one believes in childhood's many exciting dis-

Hillside homes can include safe play areas even for little tots like those enjoying this floor-level deck of post-and-beam construction. Note the horizontal-style railing which keeps youngsters from climbing through. Photo courtesy of Western Wood Products Association

coveries, he must at the same time believe that water, sand, trees, grass, plants, animals, and other natural elements contribute to enjoyable playtime. Think for a moment of the hours children can spend with nothing more than packable snow which can be converted into a snowman, fort, hideaway, castle, and other sculptures.

Sandboxes Three four-year-olds are busily getting lunch ready for the opening of their new restaurant. Twenty feet away, two four-year-olds recreate a fierce battle between prehistoric dinosaurs in a swamp laden with quicksand and prolific vegetation. Both groups of children are playing and working out their fantasies with sand and water. These two versatile substances promote instant dramatic, creative play among children. This type of play is important to the psychological growth of young children. It provides a channel through which they act out and assimilate important events. Children also are able to more easily experience intimate, interpersonal communication during play, thereby enhancing their social growth. Intellectually, dramatic play offers a means of organizing impressions at a time when manipulation of abstract symbols is just developing. No wonder, then, that researchers of child development report that raw materials such as sand and water help children develop into happy, healthy individuals who are better able to cope with the world.

Sand Sand is a plastic substance. It can become flour, concrete, steel, sugar, asphalt, or whatever the child desires. The first step for making the most of this transmutable material in your backyard is to contain it properly. Make sure that the fine particles cannot blow out of the sandy area into children's eyes. Sink the sandbox into the ground or build a lip around it. Since water is often an integral part of sand play, see to it that the area is well drained.

A very simple container, especially well suited to tiny tots of two and under, is one made of double- or triple-wall cardboard. Use a sheet of cardboard with minimum dimensions of 4 × 4 feet. Draw a line parallel to, and 1 foot in from, each edge. Now cut out the four small squares formed by the intersections of those lines at each corner. Simply fold up the sides and secure with duct tape to form the sandbox. If younger ones will be using water, line the box with a large sheet of 6 ml polyethylene plastic. A sturdy sandbox of the same basic design can be made from lumber or plywood. To insure proper drainage, mount the wooden box on 2 × 4 legs and drill drainage holes in the bottom for water that might accumulate.

The sand you put into these and other boxes should be a clean-washed construction variety, one that can be molded during play activities. The minimum depth ranges from 12 to 18 inches; kids need at least that much sand for satisfying digging.

Outdoor wood which has been pressure-treated with preservative chemicals to resist decay and insects was used in the construction of this backyard sandbox. The wood retains its natural appearance with painting. Only eight boards were required to complete the 5-foot-square unit which has 6 inches of sand atop a 2-inch gravel base. Galvanized nails were used to prevent rust stains. Photo courtesy of Koppers Company

The Canadian Children's Environment Advisory Service has developed plans for another well-designed sandpit. Their sandpit has a built-in "cake table" to help prevent overspill. Avoid flat outside edges because they encourage spilling.

Keeping the level of the sand below the edge (at least 12 inches) also prevents blowing. A step can be added for little children. Hedging or another type of windscreen may be necessary for some sites. Cobblestones or flat paving stones around the sandpit help take sand off the feet and improve the appearance. If cats are a real problem, nylon netting that allows rain and purifying sunrays through can be stretched over the sand when not in use. Never completely cover the sandbox as sand will become rancid. A hand rake or scooper permanently stored nearby is a simpler solution.

A special note about sandpit drainage. When the ground water seepage is good, the base of the pit can be brick with gravel underneath. When seepage is poor or the water table is high, dig a dry well or install a drain line.

Sand Table Sandboxes allow children to climb into the sand and are one of the best ways to make this remarkable substance available for play. If building a sandbox is not feasible because of space limitations, your next alternative is a sand table. A sand table is a table that contains sand.

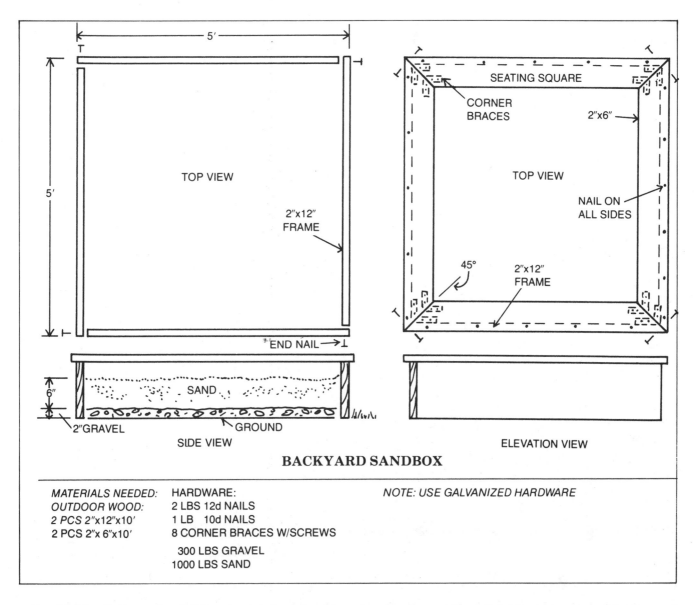

BACKYARD SANDBOX

MATERIALS NEEDED:	HARDWARE:	NOTE: USE GALVANIZED HARDWARE
OUTDOOR WOOD:	2 LBS 12d NAILS	
2 PCS 2"x12"x10'	1 LB 10d NAILS	
2 PCS 2"x 6"x10'	8 CORNER BRACES W/SCREWS	
	300 LBS GRAVEL	
	1000 LBS SAND	

Sand tables that require children to stand up should be approximately 22 inches high for children five and younger. If the table is a sit-down model, then it should be no higher than 16 inches from the ground.

When one or more children are playing at a sand table, the limited area of the sand may cause territorial conflicts. An area large enough for the activities of one child in the sand table is 18 lineal inches (in larger sandboxes, the minimum area is 28 square feet—a circle with an approximate radius of 3 feet). Children confined to wheelchairs can get to the sand more easily if half circles are cut in the table big enough for the child and wheelchair to move into.

Add a splash of water and the versatility of sand increases immensely. Water and sand together lend themselves to imaginary cooking. Supply your kids with old pie pans, muffin tins, cookie cutters, sieves, and rolling pins to encourage creative play.

You can help them make their own kitchen appliances quite easily. Orange crates, apple boxes, or handmade cardboard tables, stoves, cabinets, and chairs will lend themselves quite well to any imaginary kitchen. A stove, cupboard, refrigerator, and sink can be made from discarded cantalope crates. One crate forms the skeletal frame while slats from another crate fill in the spaces between ribs, making a solid-looking appliance. Use inverted tart pans for burners and cookie molds for dials that actually turn. Add a plastic dishpan to the sink for holding water. For added realism, hinge doors and add shelves to the cupboard and refrigerator.

Encourage diversity in role-playing with additional props: old plastic and metal gears, plastic bottles, boxes, a plumber's helper, wheels, mugs, balances, cans, hoses, sponges, springs, mirrors, and cardboard tubes.

A wide variety of props is important for a child's intellectual development. Props, such as those already mentioned, require fine muscle skills and eye-hand coordination for proper handling. Many of these same skills also are used in performing intellectual tasks: grasping and holding pencils for writing, finger coordination for using scissors, coordination for pressing buttons to turn teaching machines on and off. The state of reading readiness, for example, is highly dependent on mastering these muscle skills. Stop and think for a moment about the mechanics of reading: holding the book steady, turning the pages, and following the lines with your eyes. Youngsters who master these prerequisite motor skills will be physically prepared for reading. What better way to learn these skills than through natural and spontaneous play.

Here is a list of even more instant toys to have available: aluminum foil, ball bearings, beads, cellophane, chains, clay, clock springs, costume jewelry, hatboxes, leather remnants, linoleum, marbles, wallpaper, photographs, phonograph records, pinecones, pocketbooks, pipe cleaners, rope, rug yarn, sandpaper, seashells, spools, tin cans, clothespins, zippers, tongue depressors, wire hairpins, wire paper clips. Some of these items may not be appropriate for very young children. Parents should use careful discretion in selecting toys for their children.

Redwood boards and tree rounds were used to create this climbing structure. Photo courtesy of California Redwood Association

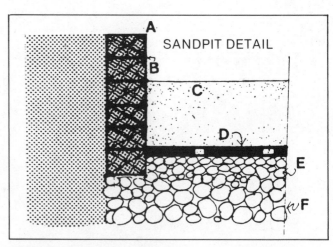

SANDPIT BUILDING HINTS:

A. *Round all exposed edges.*

B. *6″×8″ (140×190 mm) or 8″×8″ (190×190 mm) wood timber. Treat with preservative and bolt or dowel together. Retaining wall to be 12″ (300 mm) minimum above level of sand.*

C. *Sand 1′0″ to 1′6″ (300-450 mm) deep.*

D. *Concrete slabs under sand spaced to permit water drainage.*

For sandy or gravelly soil:

E. *4″ (100 mm) of ¾″ (20 mm) crushed stone.*

F. *12″ (300 mm) of 1½″ (40 mm) granular material.*

For clay soil:

G. *Drain tile to drainage outlet (e.g., storm sewer).*

Note: Sandpit can be a free form. Make retaining wall of wood or concrete with same drainage detail. Use smooth stones along top edge to give natural look. Courtesy of the Canadian Children's Environment Advisory Service

Balancing and Climbing

Tipis, tree houses, and forts inspire imaginary games and social and physical play, such as a scouting party venturing off into the dense forest and underbrush in search of wild game. They may encounter fallen logs and rough boulders to scramble over, a feat requiring balance and large muscle coordination. If logs and boulders are not a part of your backyard, it is simple to provide equipment that lets your children practice balancing and climbing skills. Balance beams can be 4 × 4s on the ground or block supports cut to hold a 2 × 4 beam either horizontally or vertically. You can also build the balance beam and support box designed by the Stanley Tool Works.

Support boxes are made with butt joints. Since the front and back pieces meet the top piece at an angle, use a surform tool on the tops of the front and back pieces to chamfer the edges so the edges meet the top pieces squarely. Set 8d nails about every 6 inches.

To make sure the slots for balance rails in the front and rear panel line up, clamp these two panels together and make slots in both pieces at the same time. Dress slots with a surform file so rails will slip in

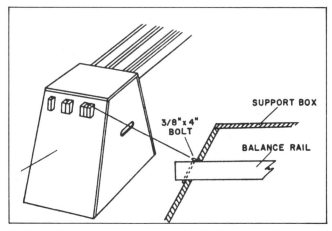

Support boxes for balance beam. Courtesy The Stanley Works, Inc.

and out easily when you wish to change arrangement. When rails are in use, be sure they are secured with bolts as indicated.

The 2×4s that make up double and triple balance beams should be fastened together with 8d nails. Age and physical ability of children determine how wide the balance beams should be. You may not want to make three rails. If you make more than one rail, be certain that only one balance beam is used at a time.

A ramp also helps develop a child's eye-foot coordination. A ramp can be a ladder leaning at an angle against a wall, a solid fence, or another play structure. A balance beam, one end higher than the other, makes a good ramp. For an additional challenge, vary the shape of the ramp making it wide at one end and narrowing it down to a point at the other. You could also substitute a round beam for a rectangular ramp (telephone pole-sized logs to tightrope thin cables).

Climbing is another skill which, once mastered, provides children with a sense of confidence in their physical prowess. Upon seeing a tree, the first thought

Balance beams help children develop eye-foot coordination and promote large muscle development.

that enters the minds of many children is, "What's the best way to get to the top?" Of course, kids will look to other obstacles besides trees to test their abilities, as many parents have learned upon entering the living room and finding their offspring perched precariously atop a wobbly pile of chairs and tables. Even homes with limited play space can provide children with safe climbing structures.

The Stegel A single structure that allows children to climb, balance, crawl, and jump is the Stegel (rhymes with bagel). The Stegel is a multipurpose balance beam and climbing structure that includes two large sawhorses, three long balance beams, two ladders, a slide, and various props. That adds up to a variety of activities for your children. The Stegel provides narrow spaces to crawl through, beams to balance on, ladders to climb up and down, and much more.

The Stegel is more than just a piece of exercise equipment. It challenges children to know and define their physical limits. It forces them to coordinate their movements in order to climb and balance their way over, under, and through the maze of boards. These activities lay the foundation for such spatial concepts as "next to," "behind," "under," and "in front of." As a prop for dramatic play, the Stegel can extend group interaction or make a story come to life.

This ingenious piece of equipment was designed for

Many different props can be used with the Stegel including slides and ladders. The Stegel is a perfect apparatus for action-packed dramatic play.

elementary physical education programs, but with certain modifications (wider balance beams and more gently sloping balance-beam walks). The Stegel can be used with preschool children aged three to five years and also can be used successfully with handicapped children, especially neurologically impaired and emotionally disturbed kids. If you do plan to use the apparatus with these children, first consult a licensed therapist for instructions in safe and proper usage.

Correctly used, the Stegel can lead both the handicapped and the nonhandicapped child through challenging and satisfying physical activities. As children progress to more and more complicated feats of balancing and climbing, they gain the self-confidence needed to tackle new and more challenging situations. Self-confidence and a good self-image are important for the emotional well-being of all children.

Tree Houses

Children live in a world of people and things that are larger than they are. They are constantly being looked down at while they, in turn, are constantly straining to see the tops of things. Tree houses turn this situation around. Perched in the canopy of a great tree, children take on the role of giants; they look down at the world. Tree houses give children new perspectives on their environment.

Indoor tree houses make ideal quiet retreats, but for one child at a time. Everyone loves to perch on top.

Tree houses offer even more: they are places to get away from it all—secret places among the green foliage. This privacy also encourages creative daydreaming and provides a cozy spot for reading. Perhaps most important, tree houses are just plain fun. Once the last plank is nailed in place, the tree house can become a crow's nest on a pirate ship, the control unit of a starship, or the castle of a mighty jungle lord.

Selecting a Tree The best supporting points are provided by trees whose main trunk divides into two or more major limbs about 8 feet from the base. The most stable tree houses are built into a tree where at least three points and preferably four of the tree are on the same level. These points support the corners of the tree house's platform. Deciduous trees, which shed their leaves at least once a year, are the best choice. The trees must be sturdy, sound, and suitable for the tree house. Most pines will not meet this criteria; they are too messy and seldom have a minimum of three points at the same level.

Once you have found the perfect tree, treat it with care. Put in as few holes as possible because holes can be dangerous to the life of the tree. There is a difference of opinion among experts whether to use nails or screws. Some advocate the use of nails because they are less rigid than screws, giving the tree some room for motion. Others claim that nails are more likely to pull out completely; consequently, three nails are required to replace just one screw. Trees which are nearing their maximum growth range are generally the strongest, healthiest choice.

Safety Considerations Whatever materials you work with, avoid the temptation to cut into the tree. If you accidently notch or tear off some bark from the trunk or one of the limbs, you can speed healing with a simple technique. With sharp knife in hand, cut away any loose bark around the wound in the shape of a diamond. Paint over this wound with tree paint specially formulated to stop decay and keep out insects and disease-producing organisms that usually enter a tree through such wounds.

Do not leave tools in a tree where they might fall out and injure someone below. Avoid standing on dead branches; it is best to remove them before starting any major construction. Keep out of trees that stand close to electrical and telephone wires. When you work high up in a tree, wear a safety belt to prevent falls. Keep clear of all trees and tree houses during a rain or thunderstorm.

Other rules to remember: 1) lift materials correctly with knees bent; 2) avoid wearing loose clothing; 3) do not use power tools on wet ground; 4) wear goggles or safety glasses when necessary; and, 5) be sure all your tools are in top working condition.

The most important safety consideration of all is

A tree with a minimum of three points at the same level makes the best site for your tree house.

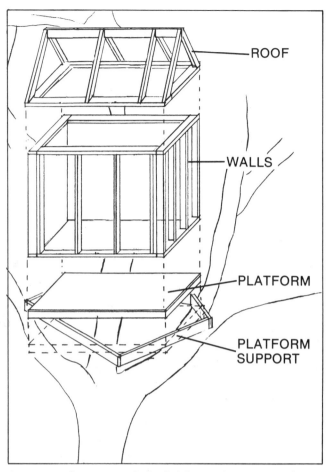

Supporting beams must be level if the crow's nest or tree house platform is to sit straight. Use a carpenter's level to check before screwing the beams into place.

this: children under seven years of age should not play in tree houses high up in a tree. Youngsters of this age do not possess the physical coordination necessary to safely maneuver in swaying places up off the ground. Safe alternatives for the under-seven crowd are discussed later.

Crow's Nest The most basic tree house you can build is the crow's nest. Named after the shelter for the lookout man perched high atop the mast of an ocean-going vessel, the crow's nest will make a great secret clubhouse or hideout.

You will need the following tools to build your crow's nest: hammer, handsaw, tape measure, screwdriver, bit and brace, and level.

The materials required include: 2×4s, 2×3s, wood screws and/or lag screws, common nails, and flooring planks (1×6 to 1×12) or ½-inch exterior plywood. (Tree sites and children vary in size; therefore, no exact dimensions are given. Build according to the size of your children and the tree.)

INSTRUCTIONS:
1. Determine the distances between the three or four points of your tree's main supporting branches. Saw three or four (depending on the number of points your tree has) 2×4s to fit the spans between supporting points.

2. Screw one end of a 2×4 beam (sill) into the tree. Now, with the aid of a level, screw the other end of the same beam in place. Repeat this procedure with the remaining support beams. Be certain that all your beams are level, or your completed crow's nest will not sit squarely.

3. Once back on the ground, build the platform that will rest atop the supporting beams. Use four 2×3s to make the frame. Construct the frame so that it rests securely on the 2×4 supporting beams.

4. Reinforce the corners of the platform with framing clips or truss clips.

5. When you have assembled the platform frame, make the flooring from 1×6s to 1×12s or from ½-inch exterior grade plywood cut to size.

   The platform can be pretty heavy, so be sure you get help hoisting it up to the supporting beams. If you prefer, however, the frame can be hoisted into the tree and the flooring added later. Once the platform is up in the tree, move it around until it rests firmly on the 2×4 supporting beams. Nail the platform to the beams with

4-inch long common nails.

6. With the platform in place, add four walls cut from ½-inch exterior grade plywood. Screw these walls to the outside edge of the platform and secure the upper corner joints with clips. Be sure to leave an opening of at least 12 inches in one of the sides for an entranceway. The walls should be at least 37 inches high for an eight-year-old. As a general rule of thumb, wall height should be increased ten percent for each additional year of user age.

Entrance to the crow's nest can be achieved by a wooden, metal, or rope ladder (avoid screwing or nailing wooden steps into the trunk of the tree; this practice may harm the tree). For example, a simple rope ladder can be made by cutting 1 × 4-inch wooden rungs 12 inches long. Drill a hole at each end of the rungs just wide enough for the rope to pass through. Tie one knot at the same spot on each length of rope, then slip the wooden rung into place. Tie off another knot 12 inches up from the first step on both rope lengths and slide the next step into place. Continue this process until your ladder is complete. Fasten the upper ends of the ladder securely to the crow's nest with heavy-duty eyebolts. Because rope ladders are hard to master unless they're anchored at the base, it is a good idea to stake the dangling ends into the ground.

Wood-Frame Tree House If the kids want more space and protection from sun, wind, and rain, you can help them build a real tree palace. For the past hundred years or so, most of the homes in the United States have been constructed with frames made from many thin segments of lumber which make good, sturdy skeletons for tree houses. In addition to the materials required to build a simple tree house, you will need 2 × 3-inch boards called studs.

INSTRUCTIONS:

1. Cut two equal lengths of 2 × 3-inch boards to run the length of one of the platform's edges. These two runners, top plate and bottom sill plate, will hold wall studs in place. Leave a space of ½ inch between both ends of the boards and the platform edge. This space will help support any siding that goes onto the tree house frame.

2. Use your handsaw to cut the wall studs from additional lengths of 2 × 3-inch boards. The studs should be high enough to satisfy your children's safety needs (37 inches for an eight-year-old; ten percent higher for each additional year of age).

3. Make pencil marks 24 inches apart on both the top and bottom runners. Assemble the wall by nailing studs at each end of the runners and then on center at each of the 24-inch marks.

4. Repeat steps 1-3 for the facing wall.

5. Repeat steps 1-4 for the two remaining sides (be sure to leave a ½-inch space all along the outer edge of the platform as a supporting surface for siding).

6. Now you are ready to put the wall frames into place. Drive 2-inch common nails through the bottom wall runner into the platform (the platform already is nailed into place on the supporting beams just as you built for the crow's nest). The first few nails should only be driven in halfway to allow you to easily straighten any walls that are out of line. Once you are positive the walls are properly aligned, drive the nails all the way into the platform frame. Secure the upper corners of the touching wall frames with 2-inch common nails.

7. No tree palace is complete without an entrance. Adding a door is an easy matter. Simply add a header at child-height between any two of the studs. If you cover the frame with ½-inch exterior plywood, be sure to cut out the door opening before nailing the siding into place. Add a safety rope across the doorway entrance. Secure the rope halfway up one side of the door with an eyebolt. The free end of the rope, complete with a safety-spring latch, can be fastened securely to a second eyebolt screwed into the opposite side of the door frame.

8. Add windows using the same procedure. Nail a header and a sill between any two studs to create the window opening. Again if you cover your tree-house frame with ½-inch exterior plywood, be sure to first cut out the window opening in the siding.

With the walls and floor complete you can now add a gable roof to add further protection from the elements. A gable roof sheds water and protects the rest of the structure from snow in the winter.

INSTRUCTIONS FOR THE GABLE ROOF:

1. The first thing you will want to cut are the roof rafters. Measure each rafter 0.71 times the width of your tree house (if the tree house is 6 feet wide, each rafter will be 6 feet × 0.71 = 4.26 feet). Carefully cut both ends of each rafter at a 45 degree angle.

2. Cut another length of 2 × 3-inch furring strip to make the ridgeboard (the beam that forms the peak of the roof). While still on the ground, nail two rafters at either end of the ridgeboard.

3. Using all the help you can muster, raise the ridgeboard and four rafters. Once in place, nail the loose end of each rafter to the wall frame of the tree house.

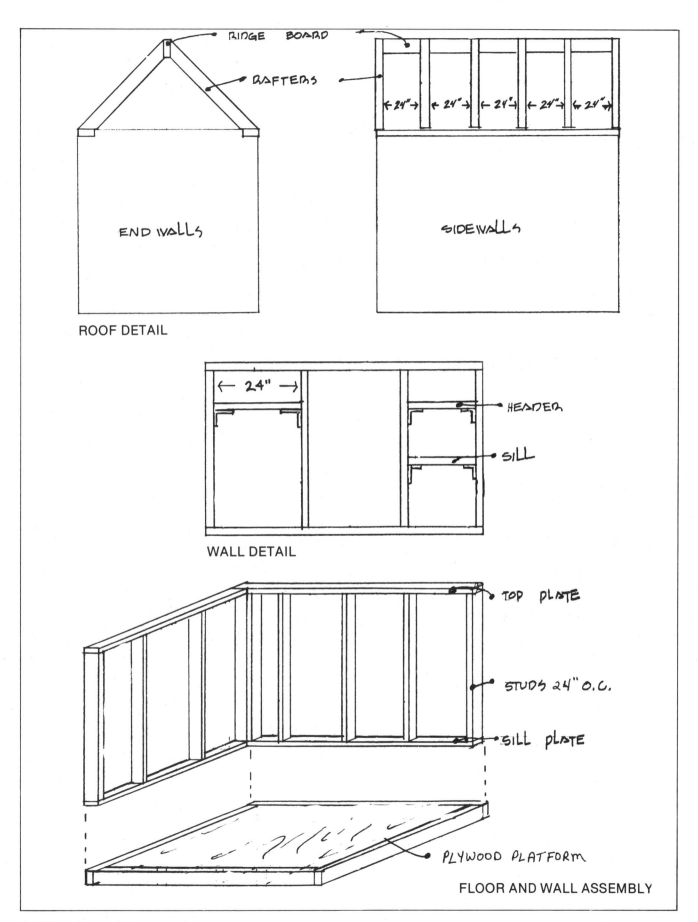

RIDGE BOARD

RAFTERS

END WALLS

ROOF DETAIL

SIDEWALLS

← 24" → ← 24" → ← 24" → ← 24" → ← 24" →

← 24" →

HEADER

SILL

WALL DETAIL

TOP PLATE

STUDS 24" O.C.

SILL PLATE

PLYWOOD PLATFORM

FLOOR AND WALL ASSEMBLY

Building the wood-frame tree house.

4. Add additional rafters every 24 inches until the gable roof is complete.

5. Cover with ½-inch exterior grade plywood, 1 × 6 to 1 × 12-inch siding, or tempered masonite, and the tree house is ready for occupancy.

Living Tree Houses Trees and shrubs can be grown to create living hideaways for children to play and imagine in.

Trees that branch to the ground make excellent natural tents and rooms for children of all ages. With the addition of props, these spaces become the backdrop for hours of dramatic play. Among the conifers, Port Orford cedar and lassen cypress are excellent. Other trees that make fine, natural playhouses include the weeping mulberry, Camperdown elm, and weeping willow. Pine trees, which are not conducive to climbing and tree-house building because of their sticky pitch, make excellent ground houses, most coming furnished with a carpet of soft needles.

Any large shrub with a branching habit giving way to open space under the limbs also makes a fine, cozy nook and resting area for children. You can acquire landscaping plants and shrubs from park and recreation departments, departments of public works or tree-service companies at a low cost. With the addition of child-sized tables, chairs, crates, and planks, these natural spaces can become the site for hours of fun-filled social and dramatic play. Such natural play spaces may be more desirable for those parents concerned with the overall look of their yard.

If your backyard is too small for this forest of shrubbery, take matters into your own hands and create a garden of natural houses on your concrete patio. You will need a little soil, several planter boxes, and a green thumb. Tub plants (geraniums, tulips, daffodils, fuchsias, and English lavender) can be arranged into little hideaways and private retreats on most patios and porches.

Planter boxes, with casters attached for mobility, are easy to build and provide homes for many different varieties of shrubs. With sturdy bushes planted in one or more of these movable planters, your children can design and make their own hideouts or small, outdoor rooms for quiet or social play. Tub flowers add color to play areas. Plants and shrubs also provide animal cover. They attract birds, butterflies, and other animals and create a good environment for showing children the marvels of the natural world.

Adventure Gardens Gardening has long been an activity for learning and emotional satisfaction. Most children are intrigued by the process of growth. With a bit of imagination, you can turn the family garden into an emotionally satisfying and adventurous play area for your children.

An adventure garden incorporates simple struc-

Low-branching trees create spaces that become natural tree houses.

tures like raised beds and bean tents and tunnels, with growing plots laid out in irregular form. The garden plants most suitable to this are common edible vegetables such as carrots, chard, or tomatoes, and enormous or unusual plants such as sunflowers, spaghetti squash, or giant pumpkins. The intent of an adventure garden is to allow children to experience the excitement of growing plants in the creative atmosphere of a playground.

Corn can be grown in confusing mazes. Beans can be grown on string frames, creating tunnels and leafy, enclosed spaces. Use your imagination and any theories or ideas your family may have.

Through involvement in the creation and operation of an adventure garden, tremendous enthusiasm emerges. If the children feel that the garden is their place, they tend to develop a keen sense of responsibility toward growing plants.

As a learning experience, a multitude of skills beyond those involved in gardening are possible. Art can be experienced in the sketching of a flower, arithmetic in the counting of seeds or the measuring of plots, music in the singing of songs about gardens, science in the miracle of growth and decay, and literature in the poetry of the garden. Discipline is quickly learned when plants die from lack of care. Cooperation can result when the children share their experiences or help tend each other's plots. Culture and history can be learned from the use of the gourd as a ladle, the symbolic celebration of an Indian feast, or the creation of cornhusk dolls like those made by the pioneers.

For best results, divide your adventure garden into irregularly spaced plots 2½ feet wide by 6 feet long. This area gives younger children maximum frontage with a minimum need to step into the planted areas.

Backyard Fun

Not all tree houses need to roost in the limbs of an appropriate tree. Designer Paul W. Mastenbroek of Woodbridge, Ontario, has built a treeless tree house out of ⅝-inch redwood plywood that gives children a unique bird's-eye view of their world. The view is accomplished through the use of four 30-inch diameter, clear acrylic domes.

Mastenbroek, who built the unusual tree house for his three preschoolers, used a 6×6 hemlock pole to support the playhouse. He set the pole in 5 feet of subsurface concrete for greater stability. The house stands about 6 feet above the ground (with an overall height of 11 feet). Children climb up a ladder secured to the pole and through an opening in the floor for quick and easy access.

Tower Fort The backyard tower fort, similar to the treeless tree house but resting on four uprights, is another easy-to-build structure that will capture your children's imaginations the moment they climb the rope ladder.

Building the backyard tower fort is an easy job when you take the work a step at a time. The drawing of the assembled tower shows how the structure fits together. The plan and elevation drawings supply all needed dimensions. The cutting diagrams indicate how to lay out the parts on standard 4 × 8-foot panels of exterior-type plywood.

Look at the side elevation drawing. You will see that the platform of the tower is built around four 4 × 4-inch posts. Each pair of posts is spaced at the top with a

Children get a bird's-eye view of the world from this sturdy treeless tree house. Designer Paul Mastenbroek used ⅜-inch redwood plywood, 6×6 hemlock, some lumber scraps, and four acrylic domes. Photo courtesy of Simpson Timber

This tower fort stimulates dramatic play and encourages social interaction. Photo courtesy of American Plywood Association

¾-inch plywood sidewall to make an A-shaped frame. Setting up these A-frames is the first step in construction. The platform is then framed in around them.

Two panels of ½-inch plywood are used to deck the platform framing. Rail supports bolted to the inside faces of 2 × 4s hold up ¾-inch plywood rails. A rope ladder hung from the platform framing leads up to a trapdoor opening in the plywood floor.

The curved, 8-foot square roof (two panels of ½-inch plywood joined with battens) mounts on special metal brackets bolted to the tops of the 4 × 4 posts. Be sure to get completely waterproof exterior plywood. Buy galvanized fastenings.

It is easiest to precut the plywood before beginning actual construction. Lay out the panels using a straightedge and large carpenter's square. Remember to allow two saw kerfs (the width of two saw blades) when measuring dimensions. While you can cut out the parts with a handsaw, using a portable electric circular saw saves considerable time.

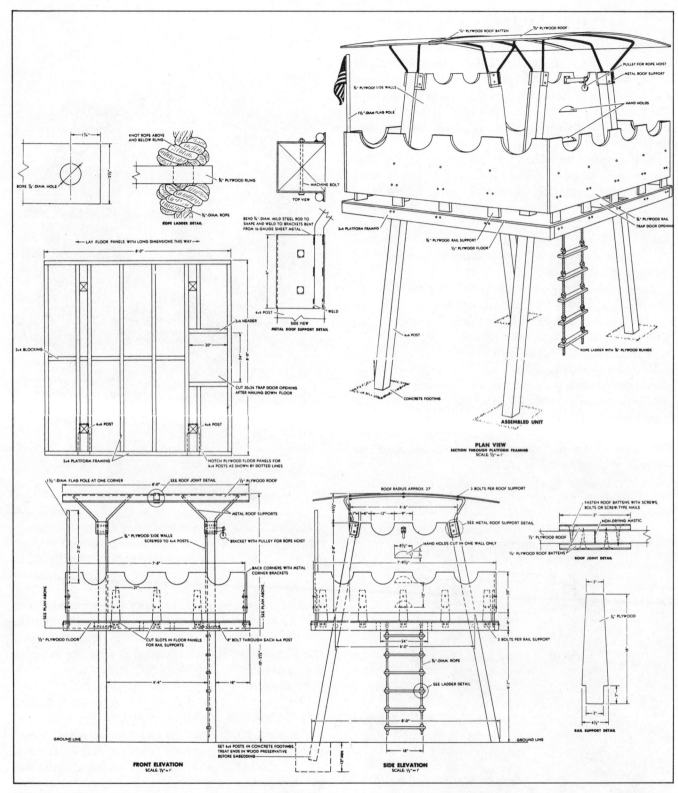

Pattern for Tower Fort courtesy American Plywood Association

INSTRUCTIONS:

1. Building identical A-frames to support the tower platform is the first step. To assemble them, arrange four 4×4s in pairs flat on the ground, spacing each pair as shown in the side elevation.

Measure down from the tops to establish a ground line, and at this line tack a strip of scrap lumber across each pair of 4×4s. Next fasten a ¾-inch plywood sidewall across the top of the 4×4s with No. 8, 1½-inch F.H. wood screws. Then bolt 2×4″ crosspieces—part of the platform framing—across each frame on a line exactly 4′7″ above ground level.

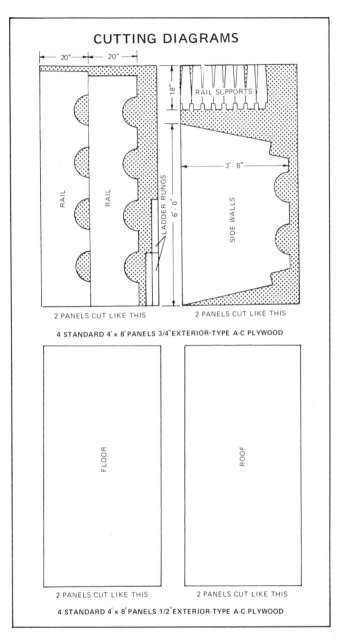

CUTTING DIAGRAMS

RAIL SUPPORTS

18"

3' - 8"

6' - 0"

RAIL

RAIL

LADDER RUNGS

SIDE WALLS

20"   20"

2 PANELS CUT LIKE THIS   2 PANELS CUT LIKE THIS

4 STANDARD 4' x 8' PANELS 3/4" EXTERIOR-TYPE A-C PLYWOOD

FLOOR

ROOF

2 PANELS CUT LIKE THIS   2 PANELS CUT LIKE THIS

4 STANDARD 4' x 8' PANELS 1/2" EXTERIOR-TYPE A-C PLYWOOD

MATERIALS

Plywood
2 panels, ¾" × 4' × 8'—Ext-ADA • A-C (sidewalls, rails)
2 panels, ½" × 4' × 8'—Ext-ADA • A-C (roof, floor)
2 strips, ¼" × 3" × 8'—Ext-ADA • A-C (roof battens)

Lumber
40 linear feet, 4" × 4" four 10' lengths (posts)
88 linear feet, 2" × 4" eleven 8' lengths (platform framing)
1 piece, 1½" D. one 3' length dowel (flagpole)

Hardware and Miscellaneous
1 approximately 9" long bracket with pulley (rope hoist)
2 assembled, per plan, metal roof supports
4—¾" × 3" × 3" metal corner braces (rail corners)
4—½" D. × 8" carriage bolts (framing bolts)
32—¼" D. × 3" carriage bolts (rail support fastenings)
60—¼" D. × 2" carriage bolts (rail & roof fastenings)
8—⅜" D. × 4½" machine bolts (roof support fastenings)
2—⅜" D. × 2" eyebolts (rope ladder)
12'—¾" D. manila rope (rope ladder)
6d galvanized box or casing nails
Screws, bolts, or screw-type nails as required

ting blocking as shown in the plan drawing.

Next, lay the two ½-inch plywood floor panels which butt on the blocking. It is necessary to notch the floor panels as indicated by the dotted lines on the plan, in order to fit them around the 4 × 4 posts. Save the pieces cut from the notches. After nailing down the floor, trim these pieces to fit against the 4 × 4s and replace them. Next saw out the trapdoor opening flush with the headers and framing.

The ¾-inch plywood rail supports are mounted in slots cut in the floor and bolted to the framing. Cut these slots with an auger, keyhole saw, and square rasp. After bolting the supports, mark and drill bolt holes in the ¾-inch plywood rails. Reinforce the rail at the corners with metal corner braces.

4. If you own metal-working equipment, you can make the special metal fixtures yourself to support the roof. If you do not, have a welding shop make them for you. While dimensions are not critical, the arched rods should align reasonably well.

Bent roughly to the shape shown in the elevations, these rods are welded to heavy sheet-metal

2. When you have selected a suitable location for your tower, measure off an 8-foot square and at each corner dig holes at least 1 foot deep for concrete footings. Set scrap lumber forms in the holes. Old boxes will serve.

Treat the ends of the 4 × 4s that will be embedded in concrete with creosote or another wood preservative. Lift the A-frames into position, resting them on the scrap-lumber strips nailed across them at ground level, to suspend the lower ends of the 4 × 4s in the forms. Rig temporary diagonal bracing set against stakes to hold the frames erect. When you are satisfied that they are accurately aligned and plumbed, pour concrete mix into the forms around the bases of the 4 × 4s.

3. When the concrete has hardened, frame in the platform with 2 × 4s, cutting in headers and fit-

brackets. Drill three holes for roof bolts in each rod. After priming the supports with top-grade metal primer, give them two coats of asphalt-base paint. Bolt them to the top ends of the 4 × 4 posts.

Join the ½-inch plywood roof panels with battens as shown in the roof joint detail. It is easiest to paint the roof before mounting it. When it is painted, lift the roof into place, bend it across the supports, and bolt it down. Dab the bolts with asphalt paint.

Fasten a 3-foot length of heavy dowel in one corner of the rail for a flagpole, and saw out hand-holes in the sidewall above the trapdoor opening. On the same wall, mount a pulley on a suitable bracket, which the youngsters will use to haul up supplies. Finally, hang a rope ladder from heavy eyebolts fastened to the platform framing in the trapdoor opening.

5. Finish your tower fort inside and out with top-quality exterior house paint. A three-coat finish (house paint undercoat followed with two finish coats) weathers best.

Built with safety foremost in mind, these swings are designed for younger children. Note the high backs and sturdy arm supports. The swing on the right has its protective, wooden seat belt in place.

Swings No yard adapted to children's play would be complete without a swing. Besides providing hours of pleasure and physical activity, a swing helps younger children develop muscular coordination and a sense of rhythm.

You can make the seat for the swing from a discarded car or truck tire. Simply loop the supporting rope around the tire and tie it tightly. You will have to inspect the swing regularly because the bead of the tire eventually will eat through the rope. A better method of attaching the rope to the tire is to fit a 12-inch length of 2 × 4 to the inside of the tire. Using a $^{15}/_{16}$-inch auger with its square bottom cut off so that it fits a power drill, bore a hole through the center of the 2 × 4 and the tire bead. Slip the rope through both and secure with a strong knot.

Suspend the tire with ¾-inch hemp rope or ½-inch nylon or polyethylene cord (these will give you a minimum load support of 1000 pounds) from a sturdy tree branch. Be sure to cover the supporting branch with a piece of scrap tread to protect the bark from the wear and tear of the moving rope.

Test the swing yourself to make certain everything is positioned properly, but always let your children have the last say as to whether the arrangement is satisfactory. If they are uncomfortable and apprehensive, let them help you modify the swing to their own special needs.

A two-tiered tire swing provides much needed support for preschoolers or handicapped children.

Movement Explorer Most playhouses function best when used primarily for social play. The Movement Explorer, designed by The Stanley Works for three to twelve-year-old children, is a unique jungle gym that supplements backyard social play with opportunities for the rough and tumble activities of growing children. For example, the unit's adjustable crossbeams are great for climbing and double as sturdy balance beams. Because of their varying lengths and heights, the beams serve all age and skill levels.

The movement explorer is more than just an exercise apparatus. It is a learning device that, among other things, can help your children acquire the skills necessary for reading and writing.

Your children become aware of their bodies through movement activities. They discover how the right and left sides work together in a coordinated way. This ability to distinguish left and right is known as laterality and is usually acquired at five or six years of age. A child needs laterality to perform more sophisticated tasks that require a left to right sequential flow, such as reading and writing.

Coat all lumber with a wood preservative (such as Cuprinol) before assembling and after cutting to size and boring holes, or you can make your own mixture from penetrating oil, penetrating water-seal primer, thinner, and boiled linseed oil. Mix together in a ratio of 1:1:1:2.

Smooth sharp corners, edges, and rough spots on all lumber with a surform tool and sandpaper. Use only galvanized fasteners and hardware to prevent rusting. All nails, screws, and nuts should be countersunk.

Before your children use the movement explorer, make sure all fastenings are tight and that there are no exposed nuts, sharp corners, rough spots, or anything else that could cause injury.

Most major elements are assembled with carriage bolts, washers, and nuts. Plans show the length and location of these bolts. Adjust the depth of counterbore according to thickness of material and bolt length. You must make counterbores before you drill bolt holes.

MOVEMENT EXPLORER

TOOLS

claw hammer
tape rule
steel square
combination square
level
crosscut saw
keyhole/compass saw

brace with ¼", ⁵⁄₁₆", ½",
and 1¼" bits
screwdrivers
surform or plane
¾" or 1" wood chisel
nail set

MATERIALS

2 — 4'×8'×¾" exterior fir plywood (backboard)
1 — 4'×8'×¾" exterior fir plywood (climbing pole platform)
1 — 1"×6"×12' (crosspiece backstop)
2 — 1"×6"×10' (crosspiece backstop)
3 — 2"×4"×10' No. 2 fir (spacer blocks)
1 — 2"×4"×10' No. 2 fir (top and bottom of backboard)
1 — 2"×2"×12' No. 2 fir (ledger strips)
2 — 2"×2"×10' No. 2 fir (ledger strips)·
1 — 2"×2"×6' No. 2 fir (locking strips)
1 — 2"×2"×10' No. 2 (locking strips)
1 — 1"×2"×6' pine (locking strips)
1 — 1"×2"×10' pine (locking strips)
1 — 2"×4"×8' No. 2 fir (climbing-pole platform frame)
1 — 1"×4"×36" pine (platform frame)
14 — 2"×4"×10' select structural grade fir (climbing rails)
1 — 2"×4"×8' No. 2 fir (tie-downs)

Hardware

9 — ⅜"×6" carriage bolts for ledger strips (add washers under nuts)
21 — ⅜"×6" carriage bolts for spacer blocks (add washers under nuts)
9 — ⅜"×5" carriage bolts for locking strips (add washers under nuts)
4 — ⁵⁄₁₆"×7" carriage bolts for top rails (add washers under nuts)
1 box No. 10 1¼" galvanized flathead screws
4 — No. 10 3½" flathead screws
10' length galvanized iron pipe 1-inch inside diameter threaded at one end with cap. Check pipe before purchase to make sure it is 100% smooth and free from rough spots.
1 lb. — 8d galvanized common nails

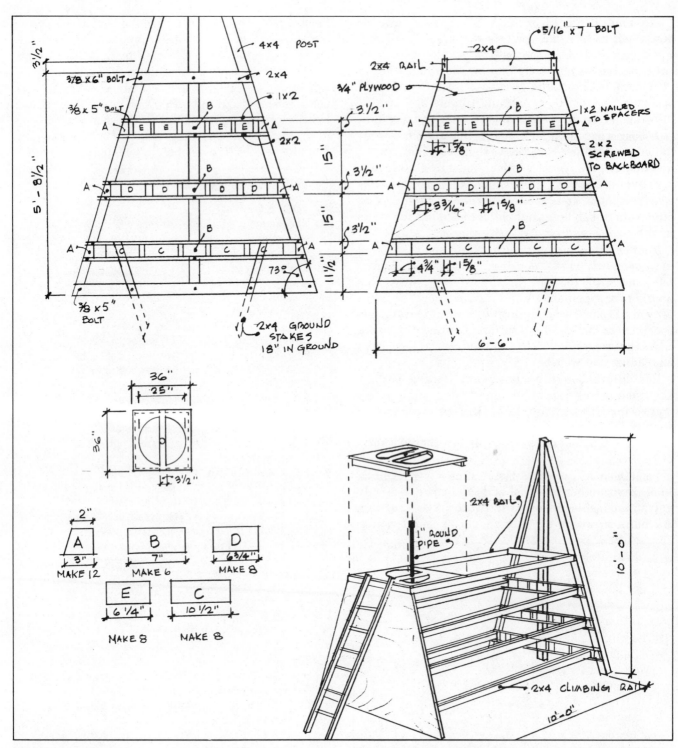

INSTRUCTIONS:

Study the diagrams. The two top rails and two bottom outside rails of this unit are fixed. All other rails can be moved to different locations in order to change climbing arrangement. The movable feature is achieved by setting the ends of the rails in slots formed with 2×4-inch spacer blocks. The rails are supported at each end by a 2×2-inch ledger strip which also serves as a base for the spacer blocks. The ledger strip and blocks on the plywood backboard are fastened to the plywood with screws run in from the outside face of the plywood. At the A-frame end the ledger strips are bolted to the frame over a 1×6-inch backstop that replaces the 2×4-inch crosspiece. The spacer blocks are held by screws run through the 1×6.

Rails are held down at each end with a locking strip so they cannot jump out of the slots. Locking strips at the plywood end are nailed in place. The 2×2-inch locking strips at the A-frame end are held in place with bolts and nuts that can be removed to change the arrangement of rails.

According to the Western Wood Products Association, a single length of select structural Douglas fir, 10 feet long in the dimensions given here and set on edge, will support 43 pounds per linear foot or 214 pounds as a concentrated load at the center. If more than this amount of weight will be imposed on the rails, double all single rails.

Construct the plywood backboard and install the crosspieces at top and bottom. Install ledger strips. Install the 1 × 6-inch backstop and ledger strips on the A-frame. Set the plywood backboard in place and install two top and two bottom outside rails. Top rails are bolted to the 2 × 4-inch crosspiece at each end. Run screws through the 1 × 6 into the end of bottom rails. Install tie-downs.

Cut the adjustable climbing rails so there will be about a ¾-inch play at one end to make it easy to lift them out of the slots.

Make the spacer blocks. You will have to adjust the length of each block slightly to compensate for variance in the thickness of lumber. Leave enough space between blocks so that rails can lift out even when the wood has expanded from moisture. Install fixed and movable locking strips.

Construct the frame for top platform and climbing pole. Use a keyhole, compass or saber saw to cut out climbing openings and pole hole in plywood platform. Insert climbing pole and drive into ground.

Even though this wooden unit is built for rough use, normal wear and tear will take its toll. A few simple precautions will add years to the life of all outdoor wooden structures. When you set units up outside, keep an eye on the weather and be prepared with a plastic cover. Long term maintenance is a matter of sanding and varnishing once a year. Smooth down the worn spots and make sure all sanded areas are clean and dry before you spread on varnish. For an exceptionally protective finish, apply a clear or pigmented polyurethane.

Apparatus such as the movement explorer provide many opportunities for rolling, crawling, climbing, walking, jumping, and balancing. Neuromuscularly and orthopedically handicapped children especially benefit from climbing, walking, balancing, and crawling activities. These children as well as blind or partially sighted youngsters, who may fall while climbing, need soft cover under and around play equipment. For a partially sighted or a physically handicapped child, normally afraid to fall, launching out through space in the certainty of a soft landing is a liberating experience. Beyond fostering the sense of unrestricted movement and self-confidence, landing and bouncing on soft material (an old mattress, for example) also helps the disabled child to better understand cause and effect as his body moves.

Nets Climbing nets also add considerably to the imaginative uses of a tree house or play area. A rope or

Climbing nets, when hung loosely, will give kids first-hand experience in the dynamics of cause and effect.

cargo net (available from government surplus outlets) has lots of physical and developmental advantages because the scrambling and balancing involves many muscles. If the net is hung loosely, its surface will change constantly as the children move about.

Climbing nets can be thrown over large sawhorses or secured to the side of any nearby structure. A unique frame for these versatile nets also can be made from discarded trees. City recreation departments, departments of public works, and tree-service companies often clear trees from public lands. If you have room in your yard, you might ask one of these agencies for some of the limbs and trunks they have removed. Sink these trees in 3 to 5-foot holes filled with compacted soil (or cement if you want them to be permanent fixtures) and build a maze of interconnecting skyways and nets. Bolt the branches together to give the maze rigidity. These reclaimed trees can be made even more interesting with the addition of platforms, knotted ropes for climbing as well as nets to jump into.

Recycling Materials

More and more school yards and playgrounds are beginning to look like the recycling centers. Tires are transformed into climbing structures and swings, and discarded vehicles are being converted into jungle gyms and club houses. In this era of conservation and recycling, it makes a lot of sense. You can use these same recycled materials on a smaller scale to create playhouses and exercise equipment in your own backyard.

Building with Tires We should be aware when discarding our old tires that there is still a lot of life left in them. With a little imagination, used tires (get them from trucking and heavy construction contractors, tire dealers, recapping businesses or wrecking yards) can be recycled into wonderful swings, climbing structures, playhouses, tunnels, and seesaws.

First, a few words on the mechanics of tire building. There are three ways to join tires: tread to tread; sidewall to sidewall; and tread to sidewall. To fasten together two or more tires, punch or drill a 7/16-inch hole through the adjacent surfaces, then slip a 3/8-inch capscrew carrying a 3/8-inch fender washer and a 3/4-inch steel washer through the hole. Secure this unit with a second 3/8-inch fender washer cinched down with a 3/8-inch bolt. To prevent loosening, add a lock washer and second nut. Use a 1-inch auger bit to drill drainage holes in the finished tire project.

A very simple playhouse can be made from bus or truck tires. Set two parallel tires upright and approximately 3 feet apart. Place a third and a fourth tire at either end and bolt them to each of the first two tires. Leave the openings in the structure's four sides or cover them with blankets. If you have a large enough sandy area, tire playhouses need not be bolted together but temporarily sunk in the sand. When you construct temporary tire spaces, be sure they are stable and cannot collapse on small children playing inside.

Passenger car tires bolted sidewall-to-sidewall make inviting crawl-through spaces. Be sure to lay out tunnels so that you have both visual and physical access to all portions, especially important for parents of preschoolers. Giant tractor tires, either upright or flat on the ground, make cozy spaces to curl up in. Stack them on top of each other, and they become a hollow mountain retreat. An enterprising nursery school staff in Los Angeles made a climbing wall of used motorcycle tires by tying them tread-to-tread with pieces of sturdy rope. Not only did this donut-wall serve as an ideal partition between play areas, but it quickly became a popular climbing structure.

Swings need not be limited to one person. With a large bus or tractor tire, swinging can become a social activity. Drill three holes equidistant from each other on the same side of the tire about 2 inches from the tread. Secure three support chains, ropes, or cables to the tire through these holes. Fasten the supports to a swivel 3 feet from the tire (the swivel guards against pinched fingers by preventing the three supports from twisting). Attach the swing by one sturdy cable to an overhang or to a thick tree branch. Be sure to wrap a section of tire around the tree branch to protect it against cable wear and tear.

Young children love to spin round and round on

Tires can be lined up for walking on and jumping through or climbing inside and resting.

revolving tire swings. Most adults, however, can take only a little twirling before anxiously seeking out solid ground. There is a reason for this seeming lack of adventure among adults. Grown-ups have a well-developed sense of balance. Our vestibular mechanism or balance center (located in the inner ear) no longer needs a great deal of swinging input to teach our bodies how to function in space. The sense of balance in young children, on the other hand, is not as well developed. The more stimulating the input channeled through their vestibular mechanism, the better able they are to learn how to coordinate the movements of their bodies through space.

Provide your children with a safe and stimulating swinging environment by keeping in mind the load the swing will be handling. If you are planning to use rope, 3/4-inch rope is a hefty size (1/2 or 5/8-inch polyethylene or nylon works well too). Though more expensive, cable is quite a bit more durable than rope. One-quarter inch cable will serve most needs. The most durable and expensive is chain (1/4 or 5/16 inch).

In some cases, you may have to sink posts as supports for the swings (where there are no suitable overhangs or trees in your yard). If you do sink posts, bury them anywhere from 2 to 6 feet underground, depending on the average load the posts will be carrying.

Additional safety factors to take into account when building a swing are: 1. The immediate area around swings should be clear to avoid any interference with the moving swing; 2. The bottom of the swing should be no more than 3 feet off the ground; 3. Exposed cable ends should be wrapped with a protective covering such as cloth tape.

You can stretch the life of tires a long way; the same is true for inner tubes. We generally think of them as inexpensive life rafts for swimming. These inflatable rubber donuts also make excellent play objects for use on solid ground. Bouncing on them, rolling over them, or using them as a dynamic circular group bench are a few of the possibilities. Why not lash three or four together with surgical tubing and create an elastic "barrel" to roll around in? Your kids will come up with many more ideas. Just be sure that the tube's valve stem is padded or deflected in some way so that it does not harm anyone.

More Buildable Expendables Cable spools are those large wooden cylinders ropes and wire are stored on. Occasionally contractors will discard the spools at their building sites, leaving them for the clean-up crew to dispose of. Sometimes old, faulty spools can be obtained directly from the utility company. Industrial hardware dealers also may have several discards ready for pickup.

When left standing upright, spools are natural climbing structures. With several units of different sizes, you can create an environment that really challenges the physical coordination of children three to ten years old. Carefully remove several of the middle slats, and you've got yourself an entrance to a cozy, cylinder house. The bigger the spool, the bigger the house.

Once the children have moved into their spool playhouse, they will need something in which to store their treasures. A functional storage chest consists of nothing more than a large upright box. Inside are stacked shoeboxes that have the outward-facing ends cut off for easy access. You can also nail together peach or pear crates to create a storage space for valuable odds and ends.

An entire cable spool can be made into a storage space in the round with an upper play deck. Cut six 2 × 4s so that each of their lengths equals that of the upright spool, with enough left over to form the supports for a guard rail. Fasten each of these 2 × 4s with lag screws to the spool. Now cut five more 2 × 4s to size and fasten them to the tops of the wooden uprights. These five form the deck's protective railing. Add a fence to keep the kids safely contained on the upper level. The fence is rope stretched in the shape of a giant W between the uprights. Add an entrance ladder to the section without the guardrail or fence.

Cut out ten shelf sections (enough for two rows) from ½-inch particle board or plywood. Place each shelf between uprights and nail in place. Do not put shelving under the entrance ladder.

For more recycling possibilities, hunt up some metal drums. Leave them on the ground for crawl-through tunnels; raise them up on sawhorses for heightened climbing and crawling challenges; combine them with a slide or ladder; or elevate one end of the drum and use it as a tunnel-slide. Drums with sharp lips can be taken to drum companies so the edges can be rolled for safety.

This fort, a maze of interconnecting tunnels and secret chambers, has been built primarily with railroad ties.

Telephone poles lift this backyard platform high off the ground. Smaller logs create the platform's deck.

With several slats removed, a discarded cable spool transforms into a cylinder playhouse.

Safety

Smoke and Fire Protection

Smoke Detectors No children's room improvement should be completed without the addition of a nearby smoke detector. Smoke detectors are round, light-colored plastic domes that emit piercing siren-like wails at the first hint of smoke in the home. The device should generally be installed on the ceiling near bedrooms and away from the kitchen and the fireplace where they can be touched off accidentally. In two-story dwellings, there should be two alarms, one on the first floor and one upstairs.

The reasoning behind use of smoke detectors is easily understood when one is confronted with this fact: 6,000 residential fire deaths occur in the United States each year, most of them even before the flames have broken out. Fire department films show that smoke and toxic gasses float above beds. When the sleeper wakes and sits up, one breath of the poisonous fumes can kill him. This occurs even before there is any danger from flames or heat.

Smoke detectors react before there is visible smoke because they measure combustion particles in the air. This is important since the least diminishment of oxygen in the air affects the brain. Usually there is 20 percent oxygen in the brain; if it drops to just 17 percent, judgment is affected, resulting in panic and death.

There are dozens of smoke detectors on the market, and their popularity can be measured by an increase in sales from 12 million sold in 1977 to 27 million in 1981. All of the units are either ionization detectors which operate on batteries or photoelectric devices that usually plug into a wall outlet. This latter type also may be wired into the home electrical system.

It is important to you to select a model that cannot be accidentally turned off by a light switch or unplugged by a child. It is also important to regularly check any battery to be certain it has not gone dead. Some of the detectors have devices that show that the batteries are working.

Portable Ladders Portable fire escapes are available from a number of manufacturers; the best feature all-steel construction and provide good support and fire resistance. Fire-escape ladders are usually made of heavy steel link, with steel rungs that are placed about 18 inches apart. Two hooks hang over the windowsill and help keep the ladder away from the burning building. The hooks fold for easy storage of the ladder under a bed or on the floor of a closet. Sit down with your children and explain precisely what each member of the family should do in case of a fire when each second is important.

Precautions with Poisons

Thousands of children are killed or seriously injured each year in home accidents. One potentially dangerous place in the house, especially for children under four years of age, is the bathroom because that is where the medicine cabinet is located. Several hundred children die each year from poisoning. Kitchens often also contain many toxic items.

The U.S. Public Health Service lists these items as the principal killers of young children: aspirin, bleach, insecticides, soaps and detergents, and vitamins and iron preparations. Be sure that all bottles are accurately labeled and placed out of the child's reach. Read all labels carefully before using.

Prevention of Electrical Hazards

Electrical shocks are another child (as well as adult) hazard, especially in the bathroom where a person taking a bath or shower could make contact with a plug-in radio, hair dryer, or other appliance connected to an outlet. Outlets should be as far away from water and pipes as possible, and no electrical appliance should be used while bathing. Carpeting, rather than bare floor, also helps prevent electrical shock.

Extension cords are a common attraction for young children who put the cords into their mouths and receive burns. These wires should never be installed under carpet and, if you must use them in a child-accessible place, cover unused outlets with plugs or electrical tape to prevent accidental insertion of shock-producing objects. Floor-level and child-accessible unused wall outlets should be safeguarded by inserting plastic plugs, available at your local hardware store.

Bathroom Safety

The bathroom is such a familiar area of the house that we all tend to forget it can also be one of the most dangerous. Falls, burns, cuts, electrocutions are all possible.

The National Safety Council warns that tile floors

are a real threat when wet. Keep them wiped dry and use a nonskid mat on the floor, especially near the tub or shower where there is likely to be water on the floor. Foam-back carpeting is especially recommended for bathroom floors; it is soft underfoot, prevents slipping, and can be easily removed for cleaning.

Manufacturers are now producing bathtubs with permanent nonslip surfaces, but bathroom fixtures last for many years and millions of homes have only the old type of tub with slippery porcelain enamel underfoot. Some type of nonskid mat or surface should be provided, along with sturdy grab bars.

Burns can occur in a bathroom more frequently than in any other area of a home except around the kitchen range. The hazard of rushing hot water to infants and small children is notorious as a cause of death and disfigurement. Adults can suffer also, especially where a too-narrow shower pipe can cause a sudden rush of hot water when cold water is turned on elsewhere in the house. Simple methods can be employed to help avoid this hazard. The National Safety Council recommends mixer faucets on the washbowl and a mixer valve or faucet in the shower. The most practical immediate step is simply to make sure the thermostat on the hot-water heater is kept at a safe level. Water heated to 115° Fahrenheit or above is destructive to human tissue.

Electricity in combination with the water in a bathroom probably is the greatest danger of all. Lighting fixtures, electrical outlets, and wall switches are grouped around washbowls, tubs, and showers. Family members using this room frequently have damp hands, damp bodies, or are standing on damp floors.

Any malfunction in an electrical appliance can be disastrous.

The possibility of shock could be completely eliminated by installation of a ground fault circuit interrupter at the fuse box of the house. These are now required in most building codes for outdoor electrical receptacles and would be a great factor in improving safety inside a house also.

Other Causes of Accidental Injury

Each year the National Injury Identification Clearinghouse releases a "danger index" based on the causes of injuries reported to hospital emergency rooms. In the most recent report twelve of the top thirteen hazards are specifically a potential threat to children. In order the top thirteen are:

- Bicycles and related equipment
- Stairs, steps, ramps, and landings
- Football activity and equipment
- Baseball activity and equipment
- Swings, slides, seesaws, and playground equipment
- Power lawn mowers
- Skates, skateboards, and scooters
- Swimming and swimming pools
- Glass tables
- Beds, springs, and bed frames
- Chairs, sofas, and sofa beds
- Basketball activity and equipment
- Floors

Index

Acoustical ceiling, 51
Adventure garden, 84
Attics, 21

Balancing, 78-80, 89-90
Basements, 28-30
  decoration, 30
  moisture control, 28
  sound control, 30
Bathrooms, 17-20, 94-95
  fixtures, 17-18
  lighting, 20
  safety, 94-95
  storage, 20
  wallcoverings, 20
Bedrooms, 4-11
  location, 8
  sizes, 4-5
  teens, 6
  walls, 9-11
  younger years, 5-6

Carpeting, 56
Climbing, 78-80, 89-90
Closets, 31-32
Color, 9, 58

Fixtures, 17-19
  fittings, 18-19
  lavatories, 17
  toilets, 18
  tubs, 17
Floors, 55-57
  carpeting, 56-57
  hardwood, 55
  maintenance, 55-56
  tile, 56
Furniture, 12-16, 70-72
  build yourself, 15-16, 70-72

construction, 14
selection, 12
types, 14-15

Lighting, 20, 23-24, 51-54
  requirements, 53-54
  selection, 52

Movement Explorer, 89-90
  construction, 90

Nets, 91

Paneling, 27-28, 59
Partitions, 30
Playhouses, 66-69
  materials, 68
  structures, 69
Playrooms, 65-66
  considerations, 65

Recycled materials, 91-93
  cable spools, 93
  metal drums, 93
  tires, 92

Safety, 94-95
  bathrooms, 94-95
  electricity, 94
  injury, 95
  ladders, 94
  poisons, 94
  smoke detectors, 94
Sand table, 76-77
Sandboxes, 76-78
Skylights, 21
Sound systems, 50-51
Stegel, 79-80
Storage, 31-49

bathroom, 32
bedroom, 31
closets, 31
general, 32
Study areas, 21-24
Swings, 88

Tile, 20, 56
Tipis, 70-74
Tires, 92
Tower fort, 85-88
  construction, 85-87
Tree houses, 80-84
  construction, 81-84
  living tree houses, 84
  safety, 80
  trees, 80
  wood frame, 82
Treeless tree houses, 85

Wallcoverings, 20, 58-61
  murals, 60
  paneling, 59-60
  posters, 60-61
  supergraphics, 60
  wallpaper, 58
Walls, 9-11, 20, 58-61
  cutouts, 11
  hanging baskets, 11
  shirred sheets, 10
  stencils, 11
  tile, 20
Windows, 30, 61-64
  curtain rods, 62
  draperies, 62-63
  shades, 64

Yards, 75